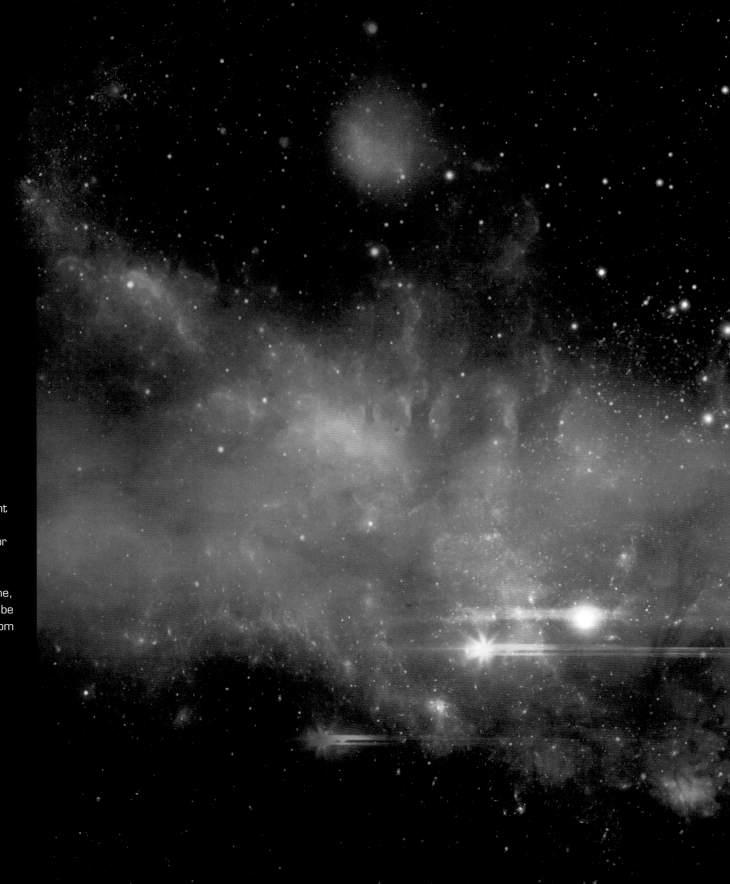

Published by Blizzard Entertainment, Inc., Irvine, California, in 2018. No part of this book may be reproduced in any form without permission from the publisher.

ISBN: 9781945683213

Manufactured in China

10 9 8 7 6 5 4 3 2 1

Library of Congress Cataloging-in-Publication Data available.

THE CINEMATIC ART OF

STARCRAFT®

BLIZZARD
ENTERTAINMENT

STARCRAFT & BROOD WAR

> "THE TIDES OF AN UNWINNABLE WAR ARE UPON US, AND WE MUST SEEK REFUGE UPON HIGHER GROUND, LEST WE BE SWEPT AWAY BY THE FLOOD."
>
> —EMPEROR ARCTURUS MENGSK

B Y THE END OF 1996, BLIZZARD ENTERTAINMENT HAD MADE ITS MARK. WARCRAFT *AND* WARCRAFT II: TIDES OF DARKNESS *HAD BEEN MAJOR HITS IN THE real-time strategy (RTS) genre, and a highly-anticipated expansion called* Beyond the Dark Portal *released to strong reviews in April 1996. Later that year, Blizzard released a game that was a dark, brutal take on the fantasy genre called* Diablo.

THE ENTIRE COMPANY HALTED WORK ON almost every other project to help push *Diablo*—Blizzard's first action RPG—across the finish line before the end of the year. It was a long, stressful development cycle but the reception was overwhelmingly positive. The game was built in a new engine and contained many new features. It was a high-water mark for the company.

In fact, *Diablo* was so well-regarded that it forced Blizzard to reevaluate its approach on another project.

Blizzard had announced a new RTS game, *StarCraft*, at the Electronic Entertainment Expo (E3) earlier that year. It had received mixed reviews, which wasn't a complete surprise for the company. The E3 demo of *StarCraft* was an early alpha build that used the *Warcraft II* engine, and the team felt they hadn't yet found the critical mix of features and gameplay that would make it unique.

By the end of 1996, *StarCraft* was still in early development and *Diablo* had already made the *Warcraft II* engine look outdated. If the company had pushed forward and committed to publishing *StarCraft* in early 1997, it would have felt like a step backward to players.

The E3 demo of *StarCraft* was put aside. The old engine was abandoned. The project started again with a new engine built from scratch. The team was hoping that the tech reboot would only take a few months, and that the full game would be released toward the end of summer 1997.

The game wasn't ready by the end of summer. Or by the holiday season. Or even by the new year.

After enduring an intense period of development, *StarCraft* released to consumers on March 31, 1998. With it came the foundation of a multiplayer game that redefined competitive gaming and served as one of the first its kind to have an intense, globally-followed esports circuit.

It introduced millions of players around the world to the Koprulu sector, a far-off region of the Milky Way galaxy populated by human castoffs, bestial aliens, and unrivaled warriors. *StarCraft* was an achievement in technology and game design, but it was also an equal milestone in art and storytelling.

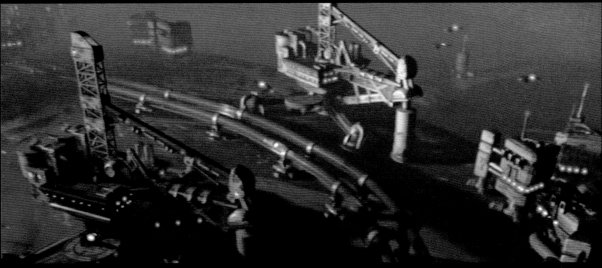

BLIZZARD WANTED TO MAKE IT CLEAR THAT *StarCraft* was different than anything they had previously released.

The game centered around three very different races who were all at war with one another. The human race, called terrans, came into focus first. They couldn't be like the Alliance in *Warcraft*, filled with noble holy warriors and knights in shining armor. Nor could they be like the heroes of *Diablo*, paragons of virtue who battled the demonic forces of evil.

"These poor bastards are cannon fodder, stuck in the middle of nowhere, and fighting against each other. They're all so, so screwed when this new war kicks off," said art director Sam Didier.

The concepts for the other two races, the zerg and the protoss, were completed in parallel with one another. The zerg were originally concepted as "teeth and feral rage," the dark side of evolution. Imagine if sharks could leap out of the water and take flight to hunt humans from the sky. That was the core of their design.

The protoss were technologically advanced, far more so than any other species in the galaxy, but they were arrogant. This combination blinded them to the harm they might cause any lesser creatures they encountered.

The cinematics team, a relatively small group at the time, began to imagine what it might look like when the three races would collide.

They built dark, isolated moments: cinematics that only lasted a couple of minutes at a time and rarely showed the same character more than once. They depicted a crew of deep-space scavengers who encountered an advanced alien spacecraft—and promptly got killed.

A terran fleet was hopelessly annihilated by a flock of zerg that sent the burning spacecraft plummeting to a barren planet. A few soldiers were forced to end their own lives to destroy an infested science vessel with the power of cold fusion.

These were the moments that made up the majority of cinematics in the launch version of *StarCraft*. There was rarely a clean victory and each triumph came at a cost, with the price being paid by the "poor bastards" who happened to be sent to the front lines.

The cinematics in the first game did not feature many recognizable characters. Marquee names like James Raynor, Sarah Kerrigan, and Zeratul were nowhere to be found. The voice of Arcturus Mengsk was heard in one cinematic, and the protoss hero Tassadar had a spectacular send-off at the end of the protoss campaign, but the rest were absent. The reason for this was simple: those characters did not exist when the cinematics were being made.

"We built characters as we needed them," said lead writer and designer, Chris Metzen. "Ol' Jimmy Raynor came to be because it felt boring to play through the campaign without a character in the fight you cared about. It was boring to hear him talk to himself, so we gave him allies. That led to Kerrigan."

A tumultuous, twisting tale of war and betrayal marked the story of the terran campaign. But once it was done, how could the story continue in the zerg campaign? There were only a few sentient creatures in the Swarm and their leader, the Overmind, was not exactly the charming sort.

The answer came by revisiting some of the terran campaign's story beats and rethinking their consequences.

"We originally thought Kerrigan was dead, and I mean dead-dead, after Mengsk betrayed her," said Chris Metzen. "When we built the zerg storyline we needed a character to care about, so we started talking: What if Kerrigan survived and was captured by the zerg? What if she became their queen? What would she do to her old friends and enemies? It felt so crazy that we couldn't help but run with it."

Though the zerg campaign did tangle with the terrans, the overall story direction targeted the third race in the Koprulu sector: the protoss.

THE CINEMATIC ART OF **STARCRAFT**

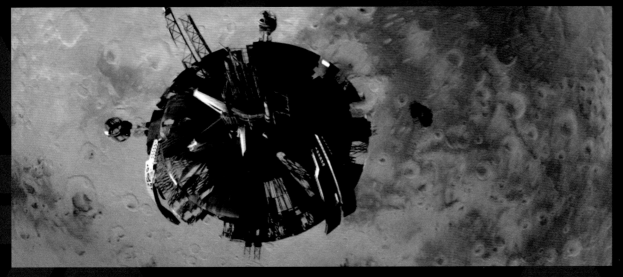

The player would interact with the proud race of warriors by witnessing their downfall. The star-spanning empire of the Firstborn was brought to ruin by the zerg Swarm. The entire species only avoided annihilation because of a hero named Tassadar who confronted the sins of his own kind . . . and sacrificed his life to do it.

Before the game even launched, Blizzard began work on the expansion, *StarCraft: Brood War*. The multiplayer gameplay was so fleshed out that even twenty years later professional players were able to discover new strategies in matchups.

When it came to the expansion's story, the cinematics team was now in sync with the game's designers and artists. Unlike last time, they weren't dangerously ahead of the curve and forced to focus on tone because the plot was still in flux.

The first cinematic of *Brood War* was a savage depiction of futuristic trench warfare. Frontline grunts with rapidly diminishing ammo stores engaged in point-blank combat with zerglings and hydralisks. It even had fellow terrans fall to friendly fire.

Above the blood and mud flew a battlecruiser that belonged to the United Earth Directorate (UED), a new terran faction bent on conquering that region of the galaxy. Contrasting the calm, soothing music of Admiral DuGalle's opulent quarters with the screaming horror on the ground, this cinematic ended with the battlecruiser flying away without offering aid to the few surviving marines left to die.

Thus, began the story. And after all the campaign's twists, turns, and betrayals, it was Sarah Kerrigan, the Queen of Blades, who stood victorious. The final cinematic of the campaign showed DuGalle's serene, lavish quarters one last time as he accepted his defeat by placing a gun against his temple.

After *Brood War*'s release, Blizzard's cinematic artists didn't return to the Koprulu sector for years. Comics, books, and other forms of media explored the story of the franchise. It wasn't until 2005 that Blizzard's creative leaders began to meet and discuss a new game: *StarCraft II*.

Like many Blizzard games, a cinematic kicked off the announcement for the sequel. The project to come would be one of the most challenging endeavors the team had ever worked on.

1

WINGS OF LIBERTY

THE BROOD WAR LEFT THE KOPRULU SECTOR REELING. THE DEFEAT OF THE TERRANS AND THE PROTOSS BY THE QUEEN OF BLADES SEEMED TO PORTEND DOOM for both species. Who would the zerg target next? Which cities, worlds, and systems would be next to fall to the Swarm? Who could stand against the wrath of Kerrigan?

But the war of conquest stopped. The zerg broods pulled back from the front lines and disappeared into their territory. Months passed. Years.

Was it over? Some believed so. Emperor Arcturus Mengsk declared the zerg pacified. He arrogantly drew up new plans to secure his hold over the Dominion and compel the other terran nations to bend knee to his power.

Others believed that Kerrigan was preparing for something far worse than mere conquest. Many who trespassed into zerg territory in search of answers never returned. The few that did only found more questions. The dark templar mystic Zeratul spent years delving deep into the prophecies of a final war that would end all life in the galaxy.

Four years after the zerg went silent, they stirred once more . . .

LEFT
Tychus, as seen in the
opening cinematic.

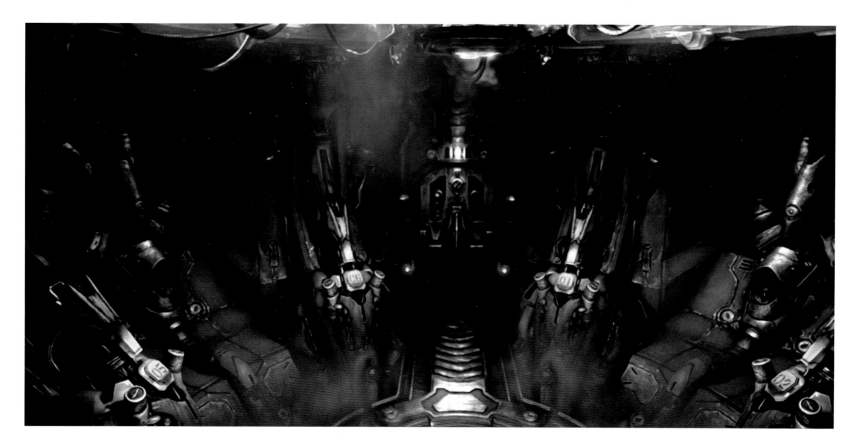

TOP RIGHT
The armor assembly room
from the opening cinematic.

BOTTOM RIGHT
Concept art of the armor
assembly room.

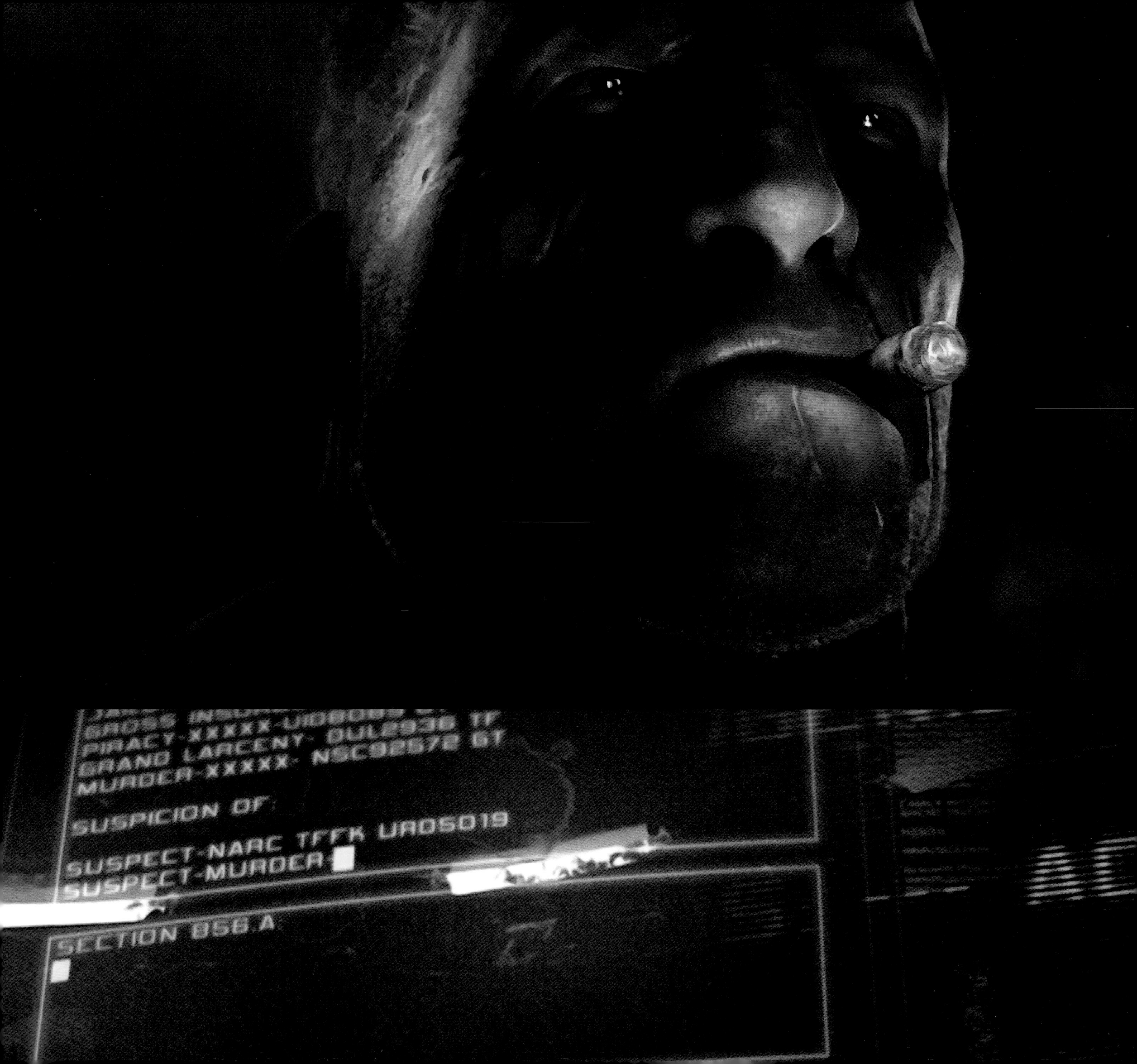

GROSS INSUR...
PIRACY-XXXXX-VI0808⁹ C...
GRAND LARCENY- DVL2938 TF
MURDER-XXXXX- NSC92572 GT

SUSPICION OF

SUSPECT-NARC TFFK URD5019
SUSPECT-MURDER

SECTION 856.A

> "THEY SAY A MAN NEVER REALLY
> KNOWS HIMSELF . . . UNTIL HIS
> FREEDOM'S BEEN TAKEN AWAY.
> I WONDER, HOW WELL DO YOU
> KNOW YOURSELF?"
> —ARCTURUS MENGSK

SEVERAL YEARS AFTER THE RELEASE OF *Brood War* the game showed no sign of slowing down. Competitive leagues in Korea attracted tens of thousands of spectators per event, and skilled players were constantly uncovering new strategies in their quest for 1v1 supremacy. The success of *StarCraft* had created a community that impacted the gaming world in ways Blizzard never could have anticipated.

The next chapter in the saga was going to be highly anticipated.

By 2005, production on *StarCraft II* was underway. As the game's developers constructed a new generation of real-time strategy gameplay, writers and cinematic artists began to work through ideas for the next step of *StarCraft*'s storytelling.

Early ideas for an announcement cinematic began to orbit around a simple in-game mechanic: building a marine and sending it out to the battlefield. For players, this was a simple action that often took a few keystrokes while they focused on fights happening elsewhere.

They had the detached view of a commander's perspective. Now there was a chance to show them the marine's side.

Inside Blizzard's cinematics team, this project would become known as "Building a Better Marine."

DOMINION MARINES WERE RARELY VOLUNTEERS.
Many were convicted criminals, hardened men and
women that were sometimes even brainwashed.
They were sent into the field and had a combat life
expectancy that could usually be measured in seconds.

Meet Tychus Findlay. This marine's history was written
on his body and was in the prisoner file that flashed
on screen. His skin was pale, like it had been a while
since he had seen the sun. He was heavily muscled
despite being shackled for a long period of time,
and his record indicated that he had genetic and
cybernetic enhancements. He even had a scar across
his belly that looked like it was self-inflicted.

"We weren't calling him Tychus yet.
That came later. I wanted it to look
like he'd rather die than go back
to prison."
—SAM DIDIER, ART DIRECTOR

The close-ups of Tychus's body were a major
challenge. The team had to experiment multiple times
with a technique called subsurface scattering before
they found a process that captured everything they
wanted. For example, they had never tried to show
subtle movements, like those in the tendons and
ligaments of Tychus's feet every time he shifted his
weight and wiggled his toes.

Cloth simulations—particularly where the shackles
pinched the fabric of his pants—also took many
iterations before they looked convincing.

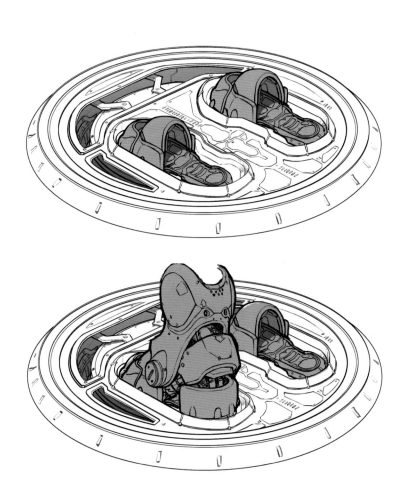

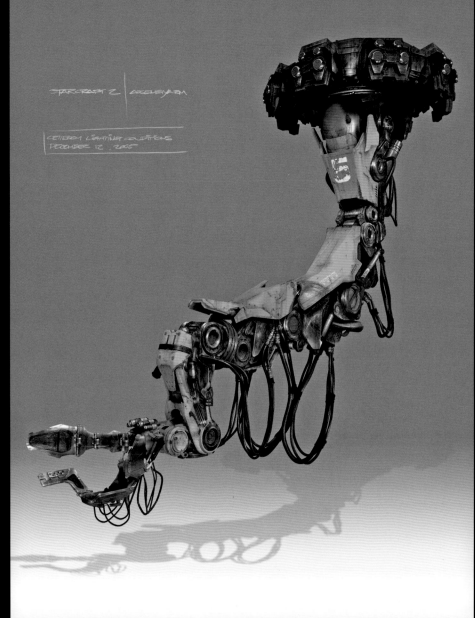

Early sketches and renders of the
barracks equipment.

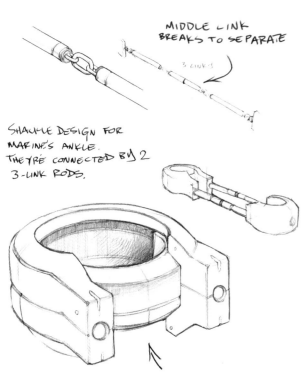

MIDDLE LINK BREAKS TO SEPARATE

3 LINKS

SHACKLE DESIGN FOR MARINE'S ANKLE. THEY'RE CONNECTED BY 2 3-LINK RODS.

SHACKLE HAS AN INTERIOR SEMI-CIRCLE RING - WHICH CLOSES IT

RIGHT
The final look of the armor assembly room and its equipment.

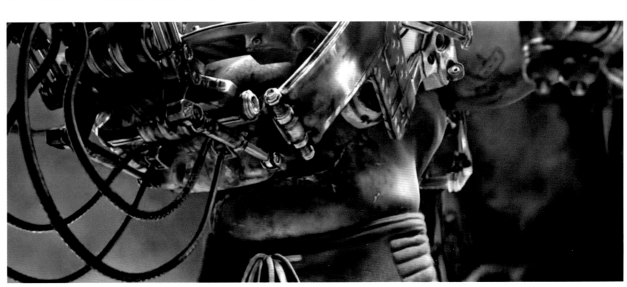

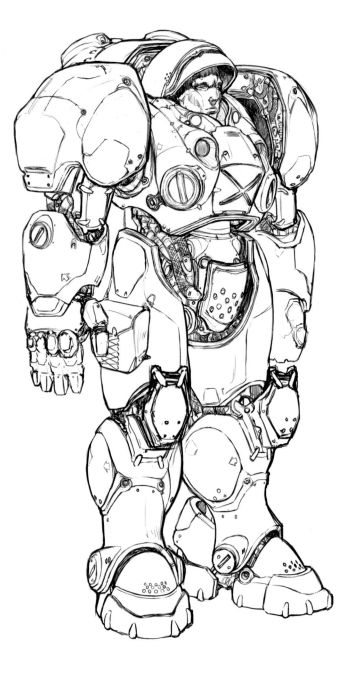

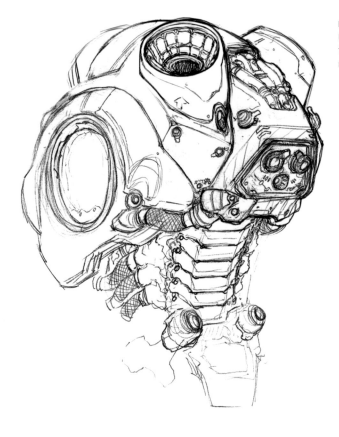

LEFT AND FAR RIGHT
Concept sketches and art for the highly-detailed marine armor.

RIGHT
Tychus Findlay, from concept sketch to 3-D rendered character model.

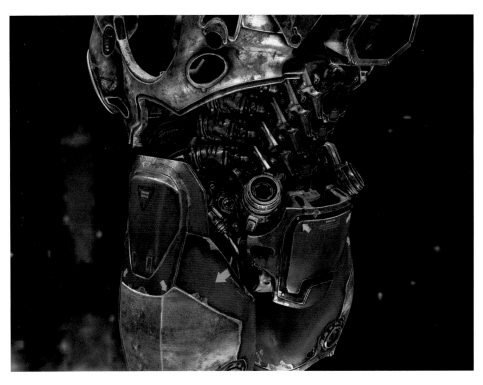

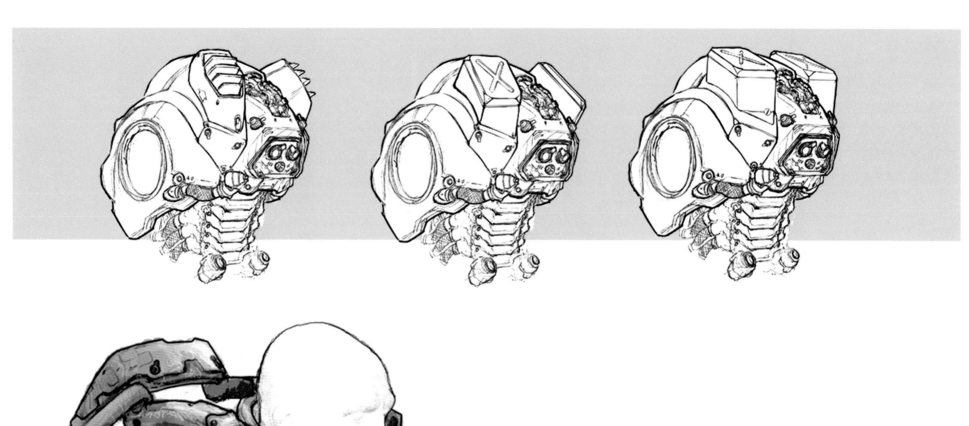

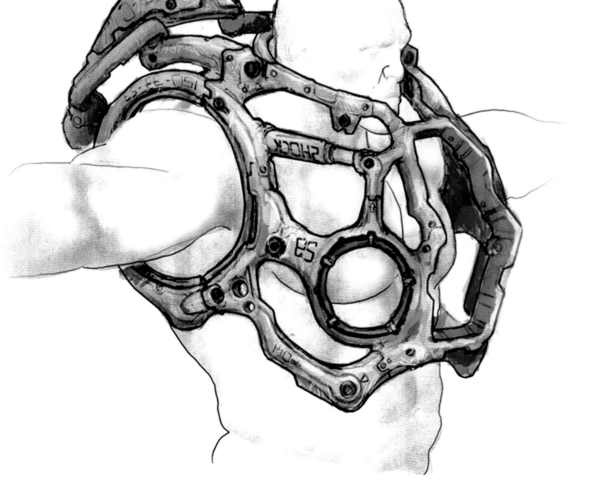

Sketch showing how the armor fits over the marine's body.

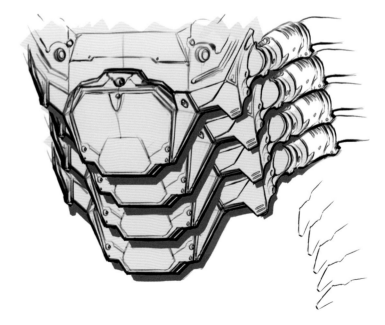

Test images showing the render of a marine suit in realistic lighting.

THE DEPLOYMENT ROOM WAS FULLY RENDERED in 3-D. The level of detail that went into the equipment and room was a new benchmark for Blizzard.

Several pieces of equipment around the room received different texturing and surfacing treatments to create the feeling that some parts of metal were more worn than others. The heels inside the armored boots looked slightly duller, as though the feet of many previous soldiers had rubbed them flat. Some outside mechanisms were textured to look like they had rusted but nobody had cared to replace them.

The outer edges of the platform were spattered with dried blood. Perhaps a previous prisoner had fought desperately to avoid their metal entombment and suffered a violent end in the machinery . . . or perhaps it was simply the leftovers of a marine killed in action who had their armor stripped off.

This was not supposed to be a happy place . . . and yet, for most marines it was probably the last moment of peace they ever had before being sent to war.

Final render of Tychus Findlay's cell door.

"MAKE NO MISTAKE . . .
WAR IS COMING,
WITH ALL ITS GLORY . . .
AND ALL ITS HORROR."
– Arcturus Mengsk

THE ARMORED SUIT WAS MODELED AND rendered both inside and out with an extremely high level of detail. At the start of the process it wasn't clear which internal mechanisms would be visible in each shot—so much more of the suit was modeled than was shown.

Many of the screws joining the armor plates together were fully modeled, threads and all. As were many of the hoses and electrical cables connected to the suit, and the equipment around the lab.

"We couldn't actually show the whole marine suit in a single shot. It's too detailed. Our renderer [in 2006] could only load two gigabytes into memory. We had to render each part of the final panning shot one segment at a time."
—David Luong, Lighting/Compositing

Once the deployment room's equipment began to attach armor to Tychus's body, the camera almost exclusively favored closeups and narrow angles. This eased the heavy burden on the 3-D pipeline. The team could strip out every part of the suit that wasn't in the shot to reduce the memory load and speed up rendering—while also showing off the heavy texture work and attention to detail.

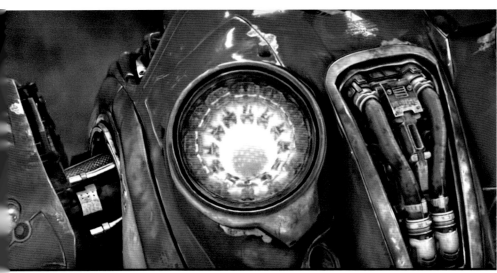

COLOR CONCEPT | SB03
STAR CRAFT 2 | BERLIEE
02·02·2006

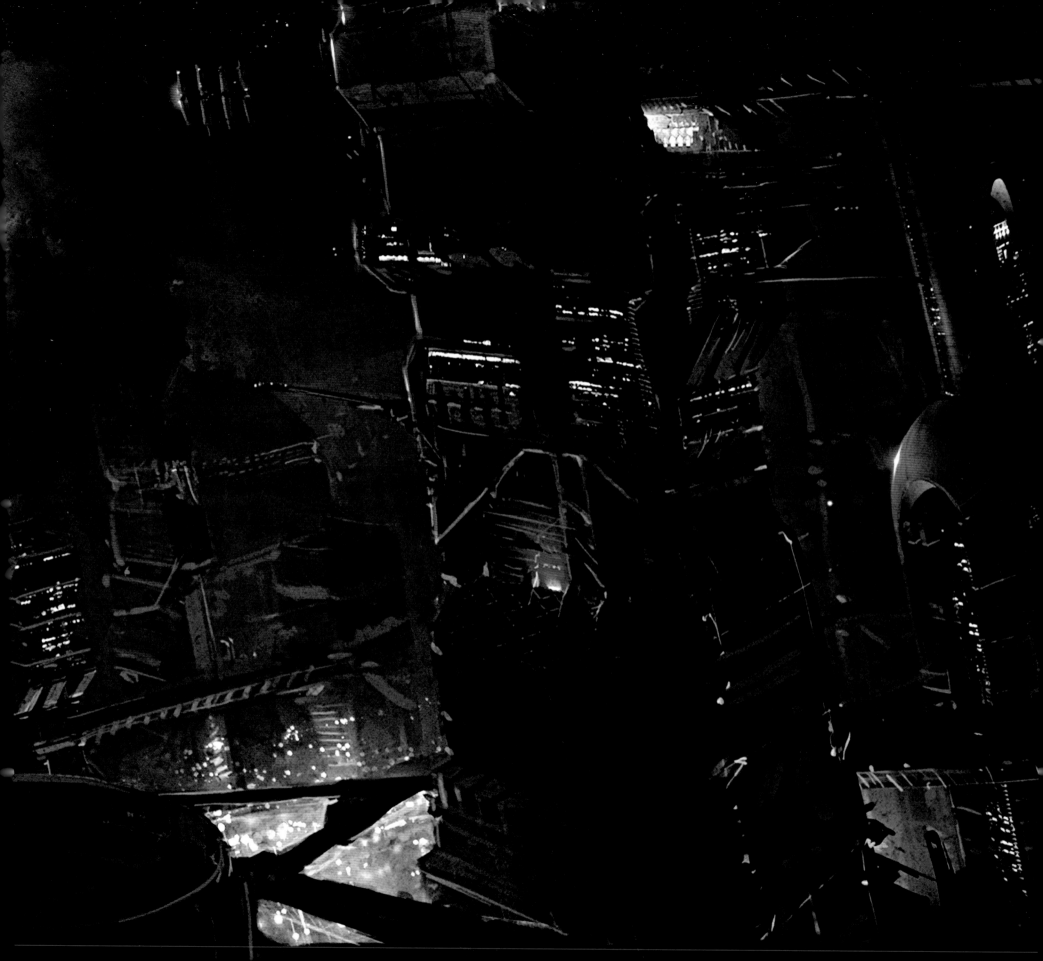

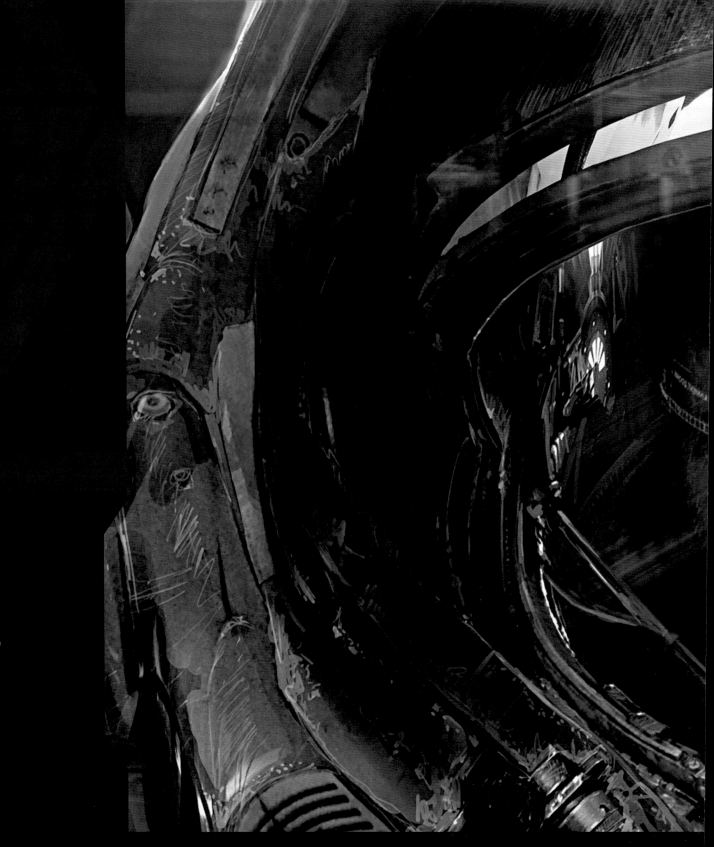

TIME"

Concept work focused on finding an iconic look for an older Jim Raynor.

FOR FOUR YEARS JAMES RAYNOR HAD BEEN
waging a fruitless rebellion against Emperor Arcturus
Mengsk and the Dominion. His old emotional wounds
were still raw: the betrayal of Sarah Kerrigan, the
woman he loved; Arcturus Mengsk, who still ruled
arrogantly over many human worlds; the Queen of
Blades, who killed many of his friends and allies; and
of course, he was still angry at himself for failing to
do much about it.

Both the cinematic artists and the game development
team wanted this history etched into Raynor's face. The
marshal of Mar Sara had a few new wrinkles around
his eyes and a rougher look about him. Whisky and
repression weren't such great medicines, after all.

These concept sketches
and illustrations became
the backbone of Raynor's
redesign for *StarCraft II*.

In the early stages of visual development, artists focused on capturing the details that defined Raynor's character before solving the design challenges of his appearance.

Several different looks and styles for Raynor. The final image on the right page is a composite of pre-rendered, in-game, and illustrated elements.

THE CINEMATIC ART OF **STARCRAFT**

Illustrated poster of Dr. Hanson
in the Hyperion cantina.

Final concept art for the
Hyperion Armorer, later
named Rory Swann.

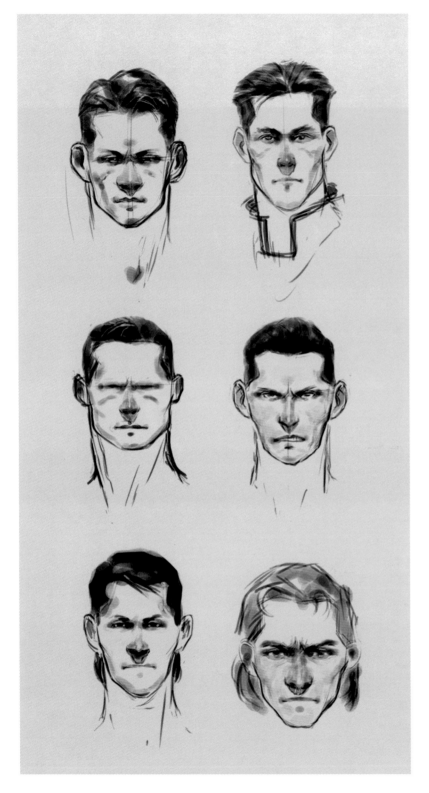

Early concept sketches for
Matt Horner, a rebel captain
allied with Jim Raynor.

Final concept art of Valerian Mengsk in his full military regalia. The left image was put in the game as an oil painting that hangs in his flagship..

THE CINEMATIC ART OF **STARCRAFT**

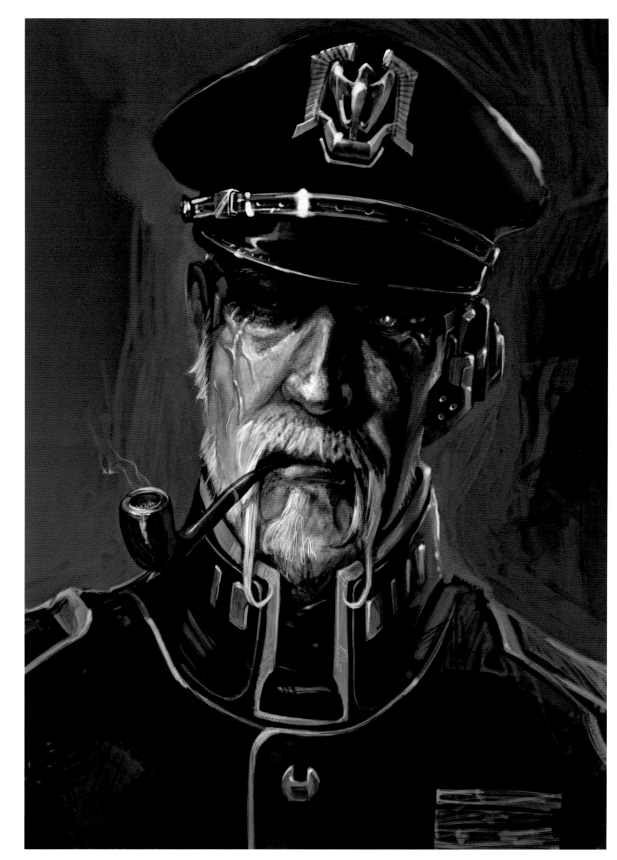

RIGHT
Concept art for Admiral Gaskaville, an enemy featured in the gameplay trailer.

BELOW
Concept portrait for General Warfield. Since he is only seen in his combat armor, artists did not need to show anything beneath his chin.

IN *STARCRAFT II: WINGS OF LIBERTY*, RAYNOR still had command of the *Hyperion*, the flagship battlecruiser he stole from Mengsk four years earlier. The first *StarCraft* hadn't explored the interior of the ship in great detail, but that was about to change.

Between missions, players could upgrade their units and unlock special abilities on the battlefield by visiting different parts of the *Hyperion* and chatting with engineers, soldiers, and enigmatic allies. All the locations (called "sets" by the cinematics team) were built from the ground up to stage the many real-time cutscenes and dialogue exchanges.

The team also created Matt Horner, Rory Swann, Gabriel Tosh, and other humans seen in the crew and around the decks of the *Hyperion*.

CHAMBER NOT TO SCALE

TWEAKED TORSO A BIT—
SEE PAINTOVER FOR MORE INFO

DO WHATEVER
IS EASIEST W/
WIRING (KEEP
INSIDE CHAMBER?)
JUST MAKE IT
LOOK COOL

FOG
(LIKE SHE'S IN A
FRIDGE?)

SEE CELL
ROOM ARMS
FOR WIRE TIE
REFERENCE

WIP

TUBES ON FLOOR WOULD
BE INTERESTING, BUT OPTIONAL
(ALMOST LIKE DATA CABLES COMING FROM CHAMBER)
POWER
ADJUTANT WIRING
SEE S. HUI'S DRAWINGS FOR SPINE ROBOT ARM
IF NEEDED

The player encounters a
badly damaged adjutant
during the campaign. On the
left is its early concept art.
Below is the final in-game model.

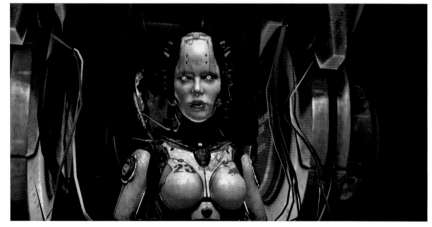

BLIZZARD'S HIGHLY-DETAILED PRE-RENDERED cinematics take significant amounts of time and resources to complete. For *Wings of Liberty*, the cinematics team delivered more than twelve minutes of pre-rendered footage, the most ever released in a Blizzard game at that time.

However, that was only going to make up a fraction of the storytelling needed for the game. The narrative clocked in at more than three hours long with all the dialogue and cutscenes outside of the missions. By necessity, the bulk of the cinematics in *Wings of Liberty* needed to be done at a more manageable level.

Four cinematics were fully detailed pre-renders, but sixteen were rendered real-time by the game engine. The in-game cinematics team at the time was relatively small, but the *StarCraft* development team also had resources dedicated to building the software features needed to make the cinematics happen.

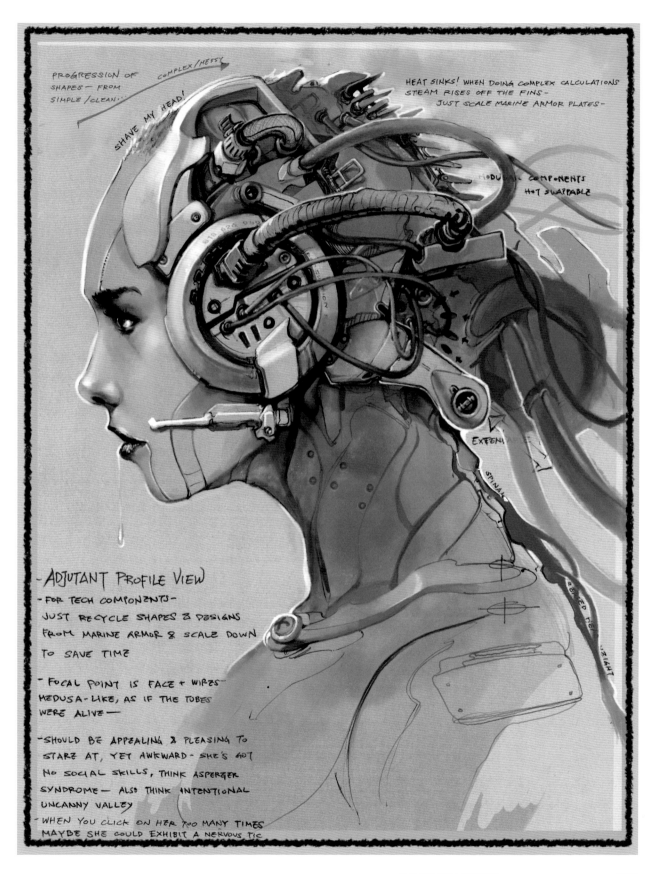

A poster of Gabriel Tosh that hangs in the background of the Hyperion Cantina.

RENDERING CINEMATICS IN REAL-TIME IMPOSED significant limitations on the scope of the scenes. Throw too many polygons on the character or environment models, and computers with low amounts of RAM would struggle to load it all. Add too many lighting or particle effects (explosions, smoke, etc.), and low-end CPUs would begin to strain.

Later expansions used a different approach. Most action-oriented cutscenes were rendered into high-resolution videos, so even low-end computers could see the cinematics at their highest quality.

Lighting artists worked with the limitation of "three lights per character," a rule they delighted in breaking whenever possible. Even so, the team staged many scenes with highly dramatic lighting sources that used harsh shadows and pools of light to accentuate the tone.

Camera angles often used a long-lens style, which made characters fill the screen and limited the amount of background that would be in each shot.

RIGHT
Detailed concept art of Tosh in his full spectre armor.

SHOULDER BADGE

SEE NOVA MODEL FOR MORE INFORMATION
TOSH'S ARMOR IS A COLOR VARIATION OF
NORMAL GHOST ARMOR

NO SHOULDER PADS

FOLLOW TONAL PATTERN FOR
THE REGULAR GHOSTS (LIGHT
AGAINST DARK). MATERIAL
WOULD BE SIMILAR TO NAVAL
DRYSUITS

CARBON FIBER ARMOR

VOODOO/TRIBAL TRINKETS

ZERG TROPHIES

TOSH'S GHOST HUNTING
SNIPER RIFLE
(420 RANGE...
LOOK AT THAT BARREL!!)

[STARCRAFT2 IN-GAME][TOSH]
COLOR CONCEPT: BERNIE KANG   BACK VIEW: BRIAN HUANG

Concept art of Ulaan,
where Zeratul and
Kerrigan clash.

"I HAVE PIERCED THE
VEIL OF THE FUTURE AND
BEHELD ONLY . . .
OBLIVION. YET ONE SPARK
OF HOPE REMAINS."
—ZERATUL

THE FIRST PRE-RENDERED CINEMATIC IN *Wings of Liberty* had been a celebration of detail. The hyper-realistic depiction of a marine suiting up for battle had set the bar very high, but it had done so in a single room with a small set.

The second pre-rendered cinematic, known internally as "The Prophecy," had to maintain that level of detail . . . yet explore something much grander.

From the beginning, the confrontation between Zeratul and Kerrigan was planned to be a massive project. Early storyboard sequences showed an elaborate battle that would easily be the longest single scene ever attempted by Blizzard cinematics.

In the end, the total length of the cinematic was reduced from more than ten minutes to just under four. It was enough time to let Zeratul clash with the Swarm, while trimming his prolonged fight with their Queen.

But the epic scope of the scene remained. "The Prophecy" showed an ancient temple, a pack of hydralisk hunters sneaking through the shadows, a dark templar mystic wreathed in black smoke, and the visage of Sarah Kerrigan as the Queen of Blades.

Concept sketches of the prophetic images inside Ulnar that show the zerg and protoss combining into a new, unholy creature.

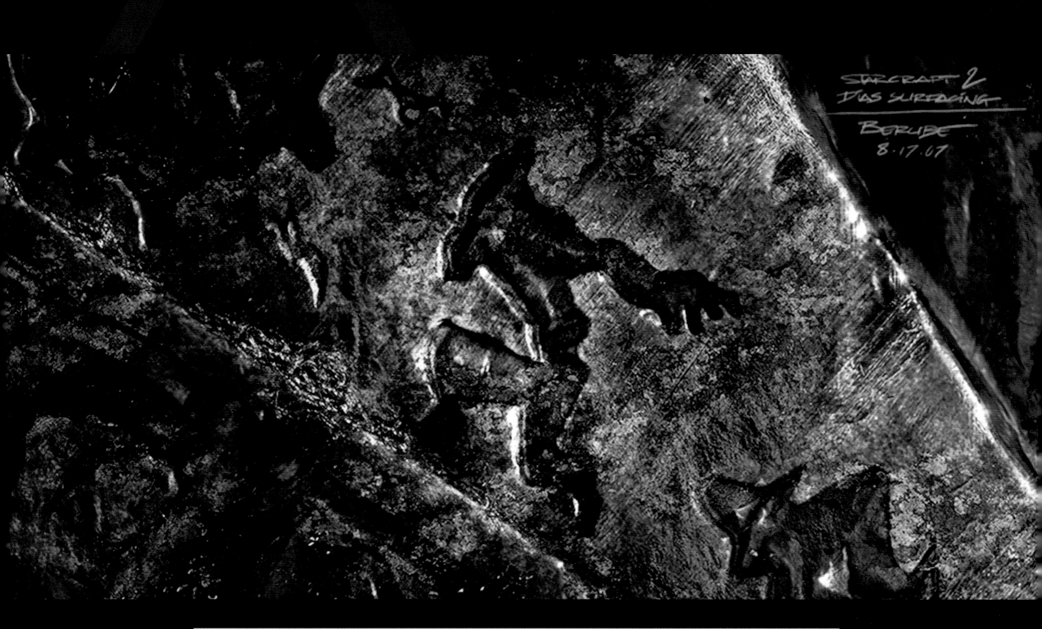

STARCRAFT 2
DAS SURFOGING
BERLIDE
8·17·07

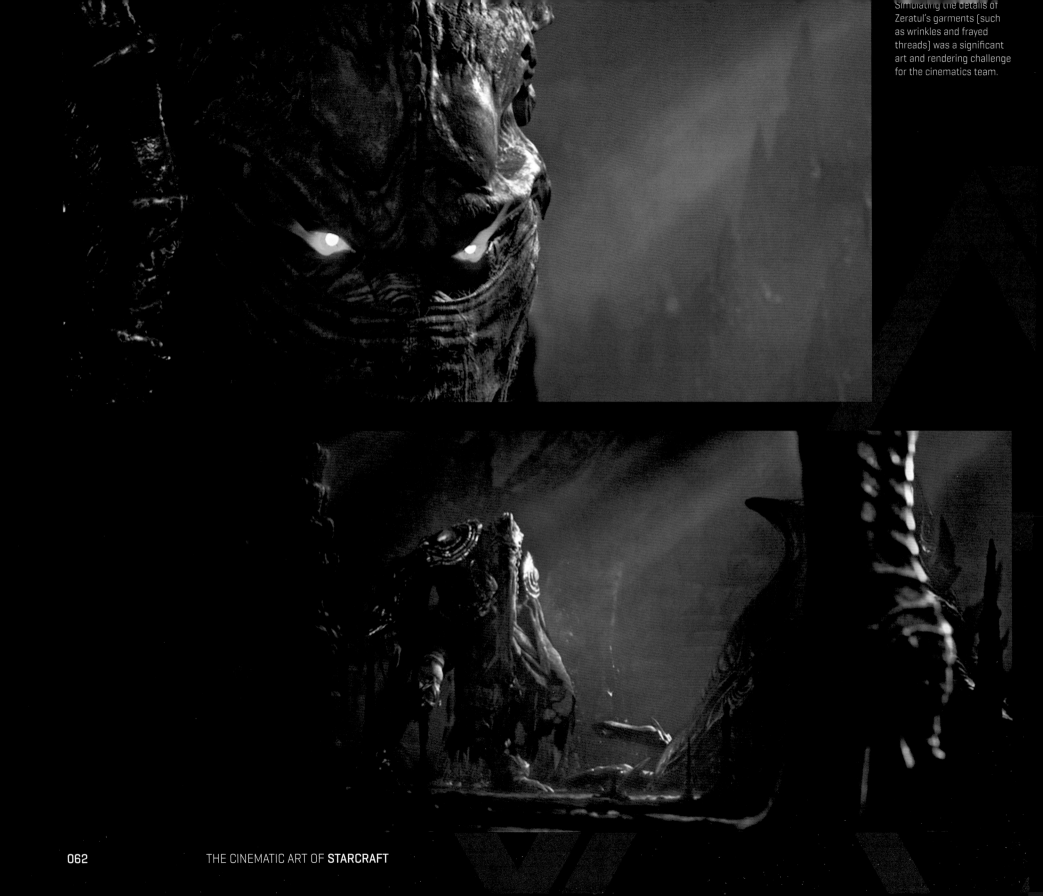

Simulating the details of Zeratul's garments (such as wrinkles and frayed threads) was a significant art and rendering challenge for the cinematics team.

The physics of Kerrigan's hair posed unique challenges which animation and design solved by imitating the physical attributes of dreadlocks.

MC94
STARCRAFT 2
BERUBE
7.9.07

LEFT
Zeratul kills a hydralisk
with its severed claw.

TOP
Lighting sketch for the shot
in which Zeratul nurses
his injuries.

BOTTOM
Kerrigan and Zeratul
mid-fight.

MOST TERRAN CHARACTERS IN *WINGS OF Liberty* wore heavy armor, and the others that didn't wore uniforms appropriate for their profession.

Zeratul was going to require a different approach. He wore little armor, equipment, or clothing, so his anatomy required careful rendering of detail—much more than had been visible during his appearance in *Brood War*.

Other than Zeratul's equipment—his warp blade gauntlet and the bandolier strapped around his torso—all he wore was loose clothing. Zeratul's fight against Kerrigan and her hydralisks required many iterations on the cloth simulations, both to make them look believable, and to prevent them from showing too much anatomy.

"Paintover" frames like these are common in later stages of the production process to improve the read of a shot.

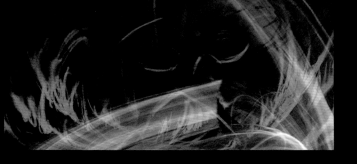

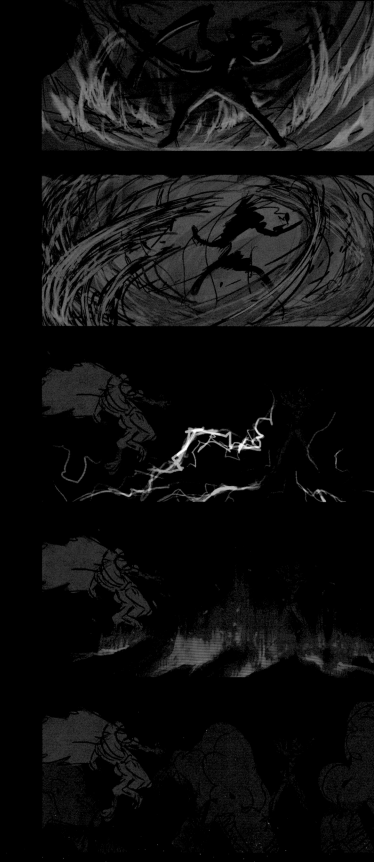

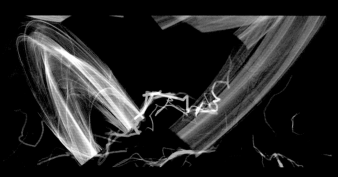

Storyboards depicting the progression of a visual effect for a lengthy sequence that eventually got cut.

THIS WAS THE FIRST AND ONLY SEQUENCE where the Queen of Blades would be shown in all her infested glory during *Wings of Liberty*, so her appearance needed to make a statement.

Many of Kerrigan's full-body shots in "The Prophecy" took months to complete. The lighting, the background, and the challenge of showing her regrow severed limbs all added up to a significant creative and technical challenge.

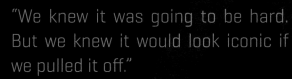

A process called pre-visualization,
where simplified characters,
lighting, and effects are placed in
3-D space to demonstrate movement and composition, was used
to stage the fight.

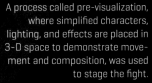

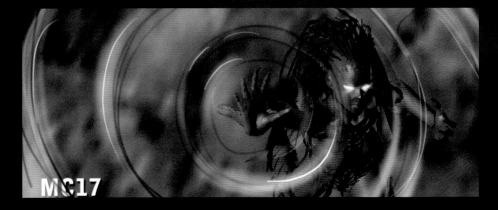

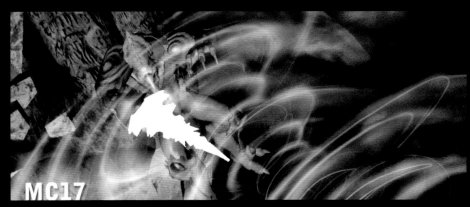

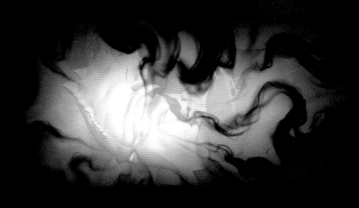

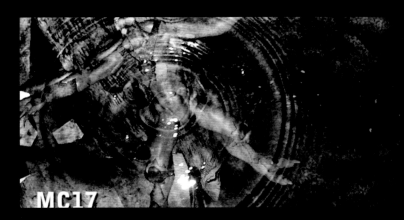

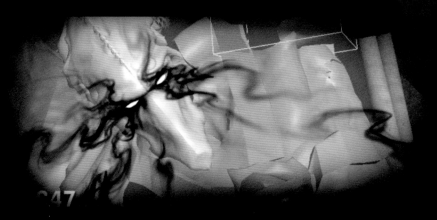

"DAMN YOU, ARCTURUS!
DON'T DO THIS."
—JIM RAYNOR

IN THE FIRST *STARCRAFT*, ONE OF THE KEY moments of the terran campaign was staged entirely through radio transmissions: the betrayal of Sarah Kerrigan by Arcturus Mengsk at the battle of New Gettysburg.

For the story arc of *StarCraft II* players needed to understand how this single moment of hubris shaped the fate of the universe. The cinematics team realized that the only way to deliver the emotional impact of that moment again was to see it up close.

Players needed to see hope slipping away. They needed to see the fury of Raynor, and the moment Mengsk made his cold-blooded decision. They needed to see Kerrigan's realization that she had been betrayed—and they needed to understand how her rage had carried through to her new existence as the Queen of Blades.

RIGHT
Concept portrait for a human Kerrigan.

BELOW
Detailed lighting paintovers for Kerrigan's desperate fight against the Swarm.

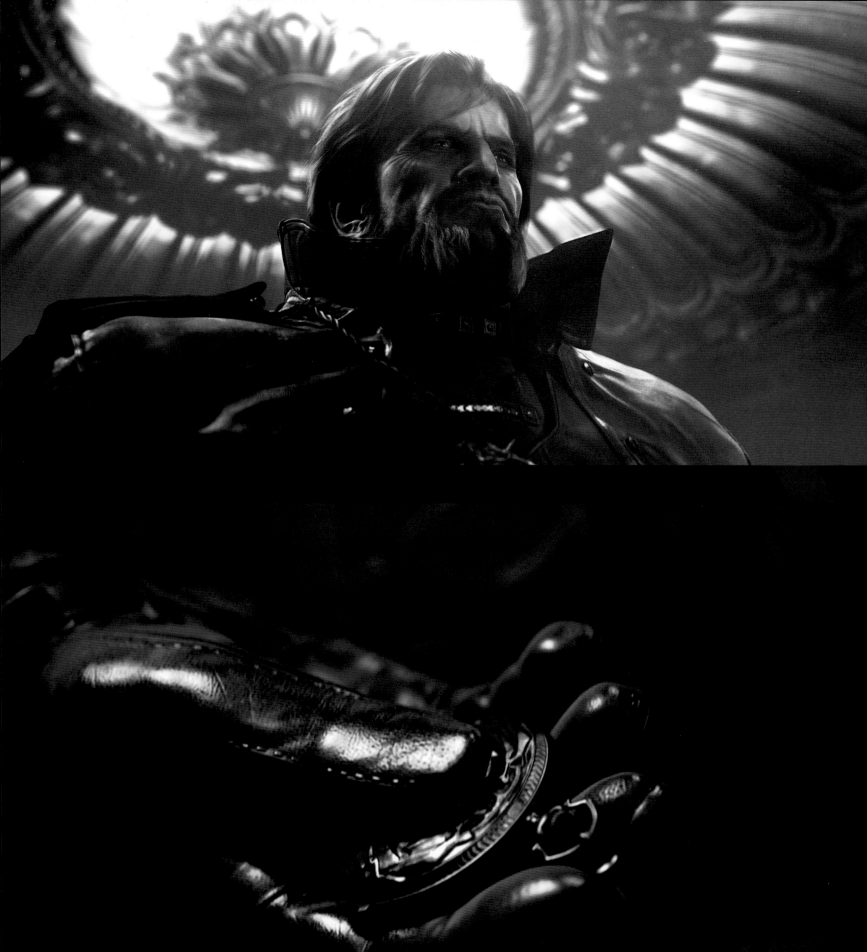

Arcturus's aggrandized self-image was enhanced through over-the-top paintings. The "oil painting" on the right hangs in his flagship.

Concept art aimed to give Arcturus Mengsk a sense of opulence and stand in contrast to the grit and terror of the war on the front lines.

The many different styles for Arcturus's face and hair. The final character model seen below is the style the artists eventually landed on.

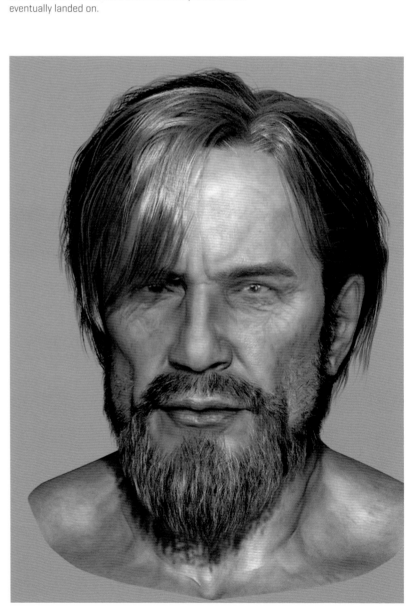

Lighting concept art
from the development
of this scene.

Still image from the
completed cinematic

"IT'S DONE. HELMSMAN,
SIGNAL THE FLEET AND TAKE
US OUT OF ORBIT. NOW!"
—Arcturus Mengsk

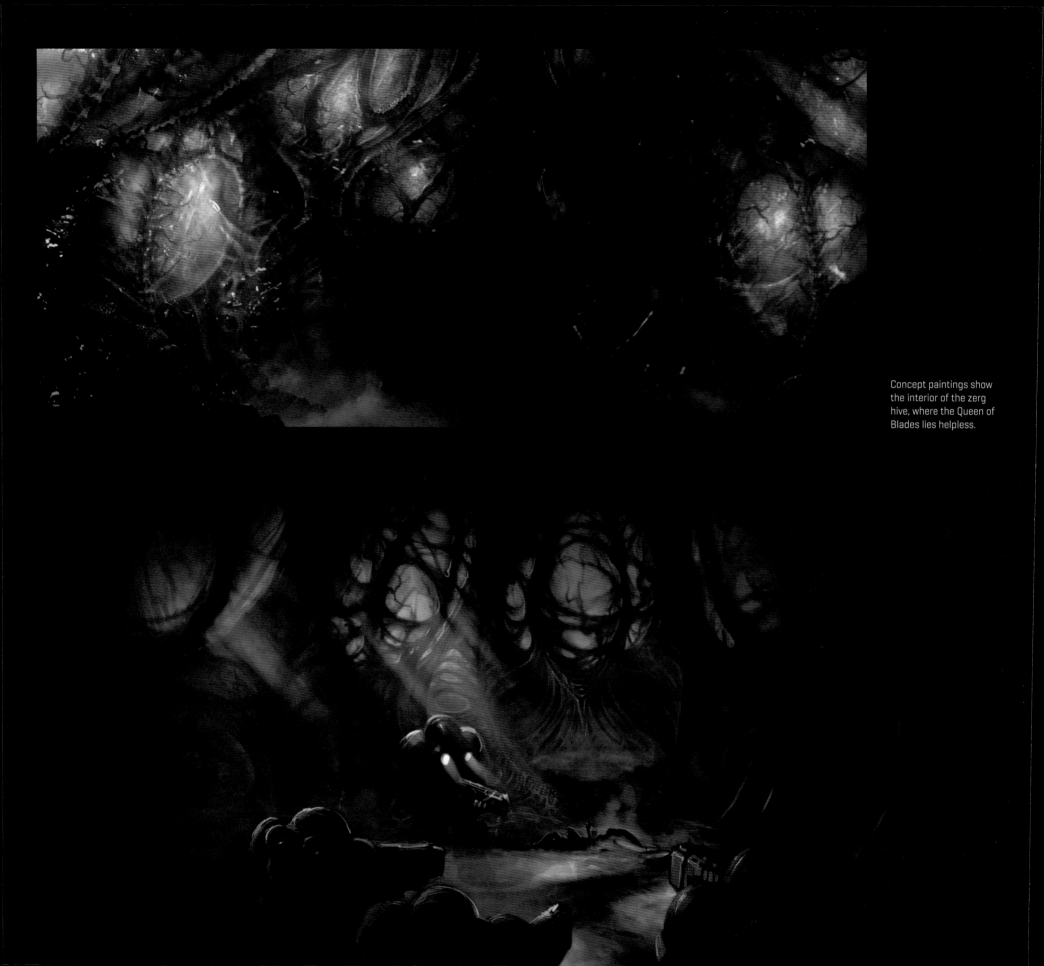

Concept paintings show the interior of the zerg hive, where the Queen of Blades lies helpless.

"WE ALL GOT OUR
CHOICES TO MAKE."
—JIM RAYNOR

THE CLIMAX OF *WINGS OF LIBERTY* HAPPENED
on the zerg world of Char, where the armies of Jim
Raynor, Valerian Mengsk, and Horace Warfield staged
a desperate strike on the Queen of Blades—not to kill
her, but to make her human once more.

The cinematic would only begin after the mission
succeeded. Sarah Kerrigan was helpless. Her zerg
went silent.

Her life was in the hands of Jim Raynor.

And Tychus Findlay had orders to kill her.

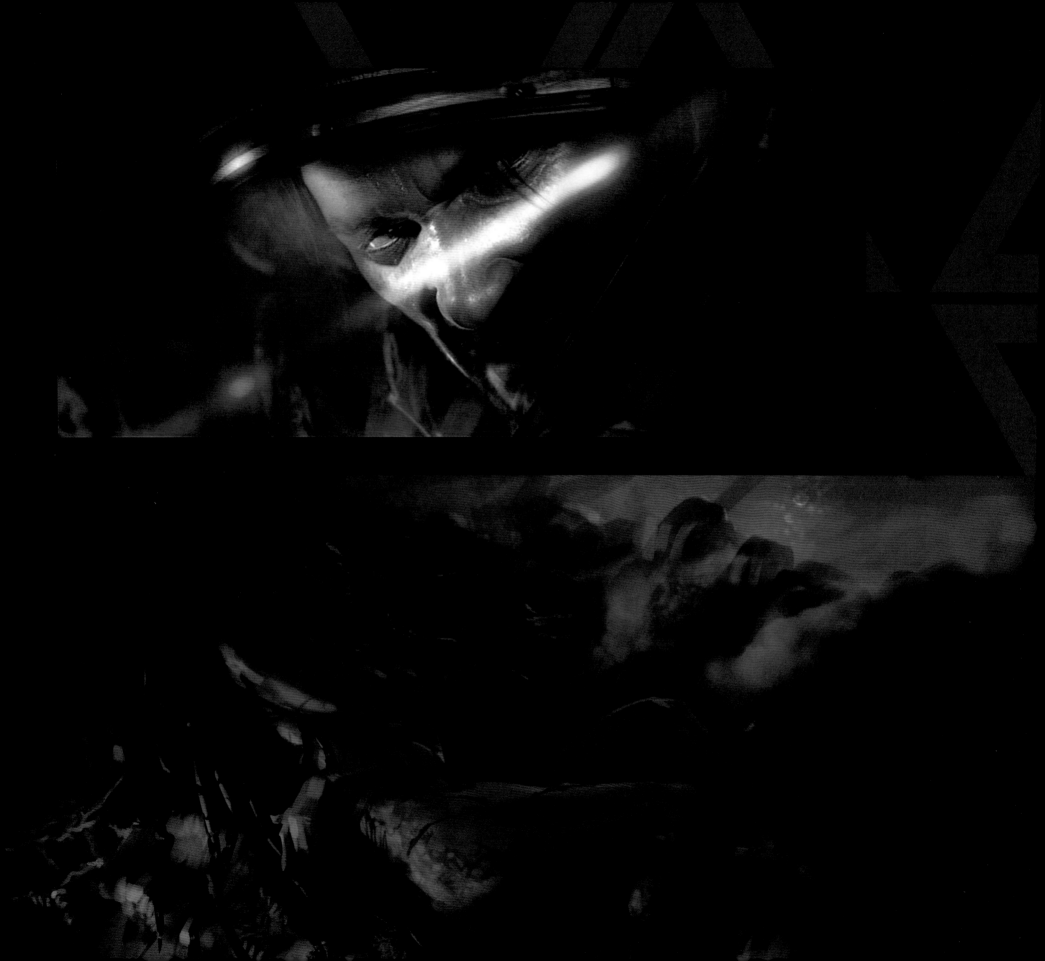

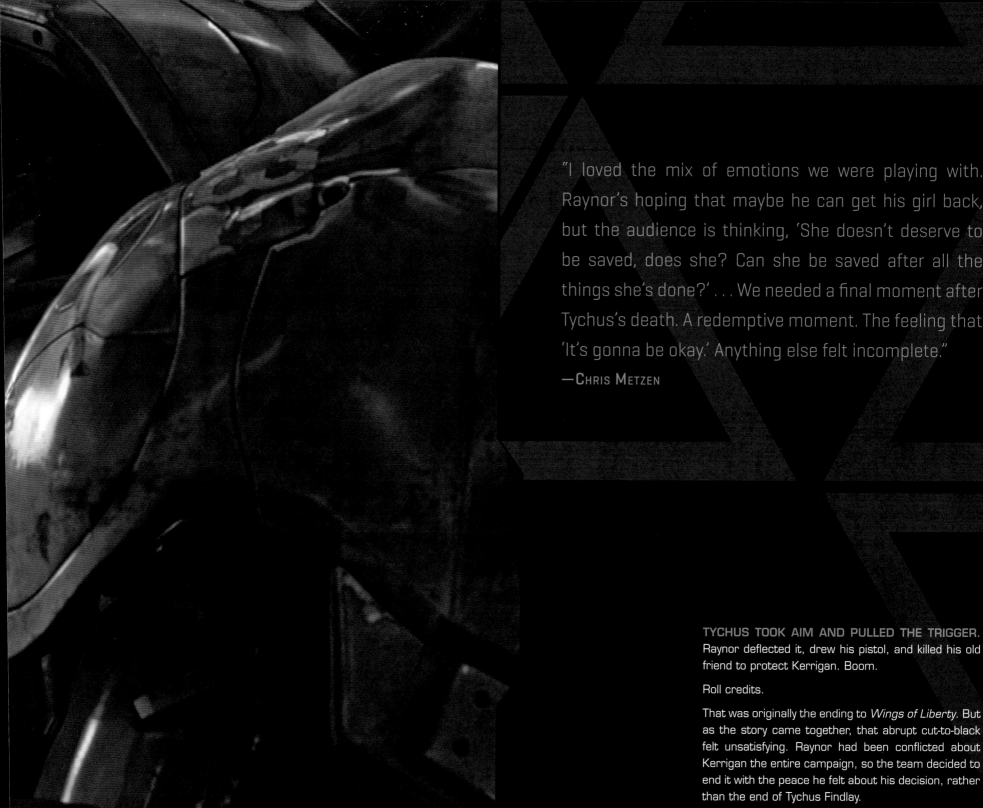

"I loved the mix of emotions we were playing with. Raynor's hoping that maybe he can get his girl back, but the audience is thinking, 'She doesn't deserve to be saved, does she? Can she be saved after all the things she's done?' ... We needed a final moment after Tychus's death. A redemptive moment. The feeling that 'It's gonna be okay.' Anything else felt incomplete."
—CHRIS METZEN

TYCHUS TOOK AIM AND PULLED THE TRIGGER. Raynor deflected it, drew his pistol, and killed his old friend to protect Kerrigan. Boom.

Roll credits.

That was originally the ending to *Wings of Liberty*. But as the story came together, that abrupt cut-to-black felt unsatisfying. Raynor had been conflicted about Kerrigan the entire campaign, so the team decided to end it with the peace he felt about his decision, rather than the end of Tychus Findlay.

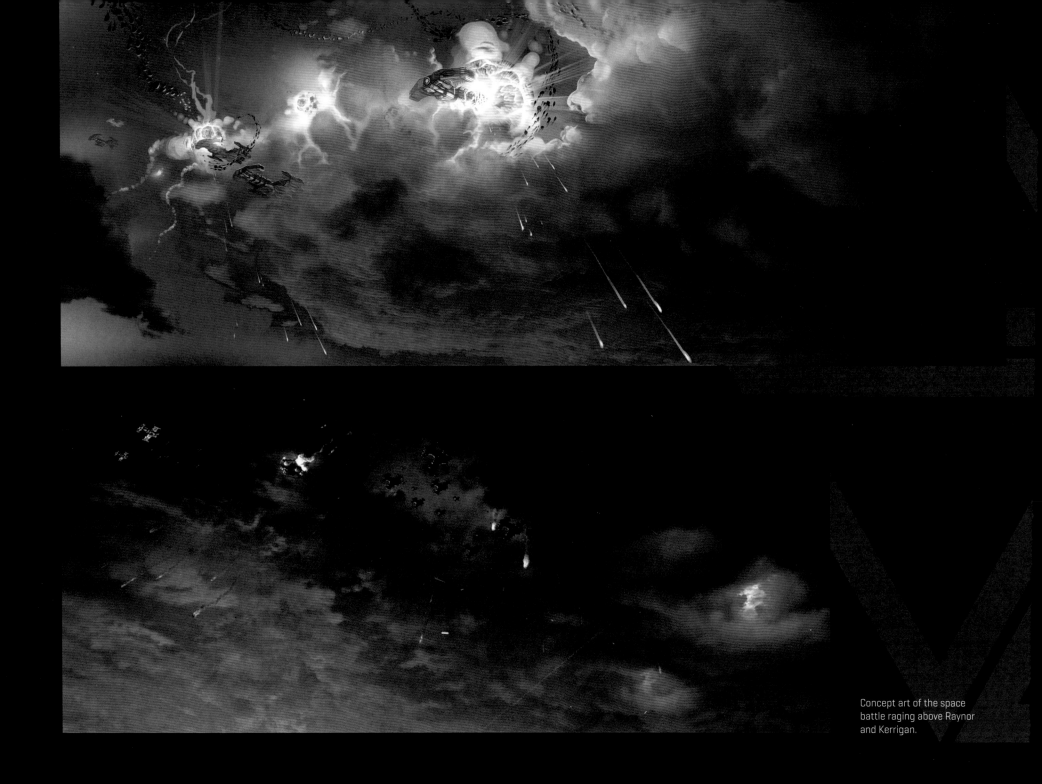

Concept art of the space
battle raging above Raynor
and Kerrigan.

THE CINEMATIC ART OF **STARCRAFT**

NEXT PAGE
The background matte
painting in the final shot of
Wings of Liberty.

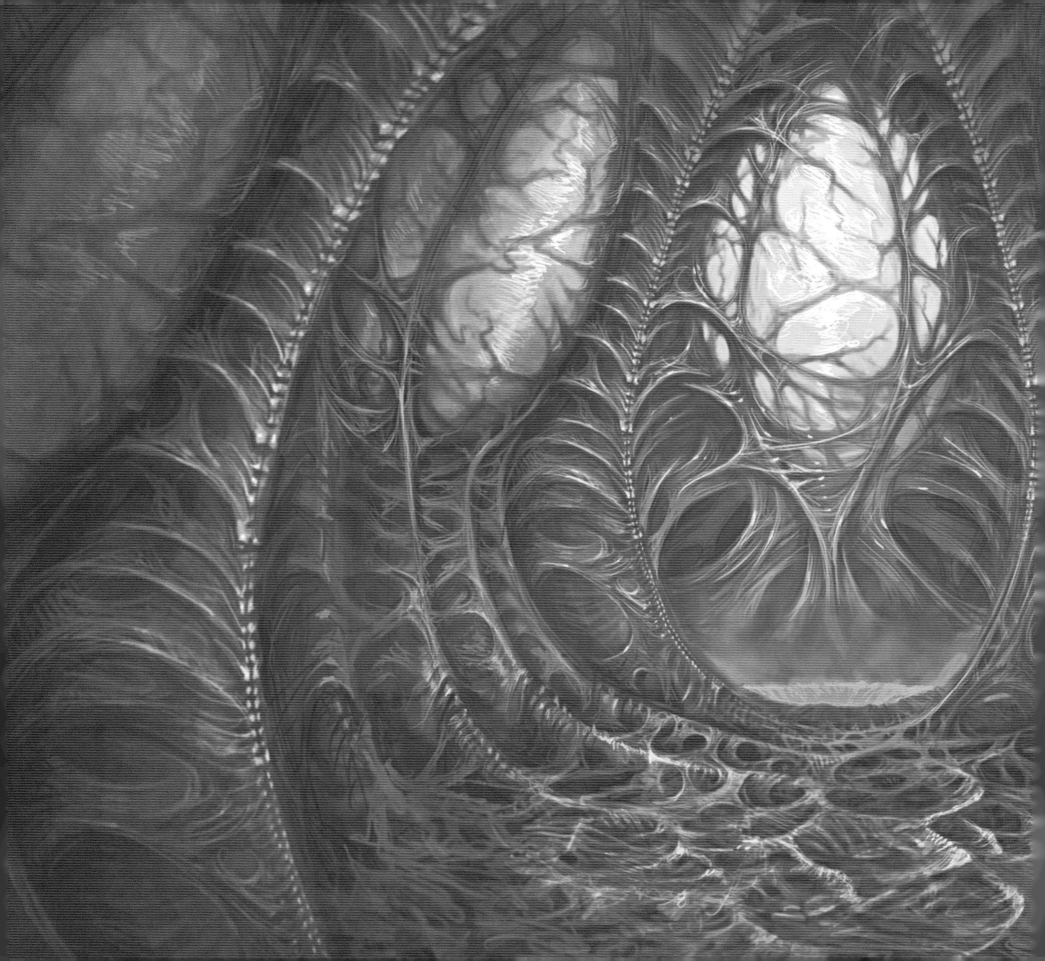

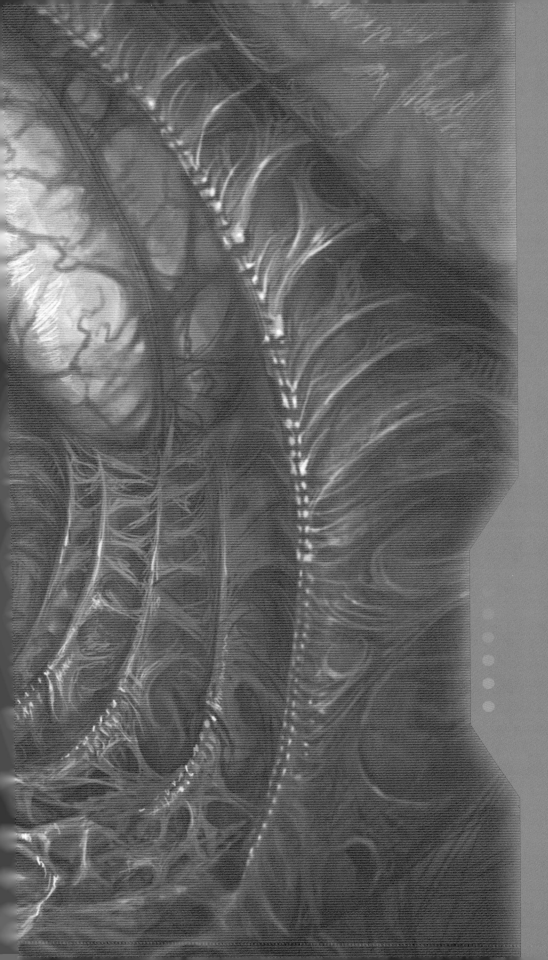

2

HEART OF THE SWARM

THE REIGN OF THE QUEEN OF BLADES ENDED. SARAH KERRIGAN, THE WOMAN WHO HAD TRANSFORMED INTO THE UNSTOPPABLE LEADER OF THE SWARM, regained her humanity. Mostly. However, her happy reunion with Jim Raynor soon gave way to uncertainty and guilt. She once wielded more power than any other creature in the galaxy, and billions died for it.

Yet even with the Swarm no longer at her command, Kerrigan's desire for vengeance against Arcturus Mengsk had not diminished.

Valerian Mengsk, Arcturus's son and the secretive head of the Mobius Foundation, offered Kerrigan and Raynor sanctuary at an Umojan science laboratory while he studied what she was still capable of doing. But this brief time of rest came to an end.

The fates of Kerrigan, Raynor, and Arcturus Mengsk were going to collide once again.

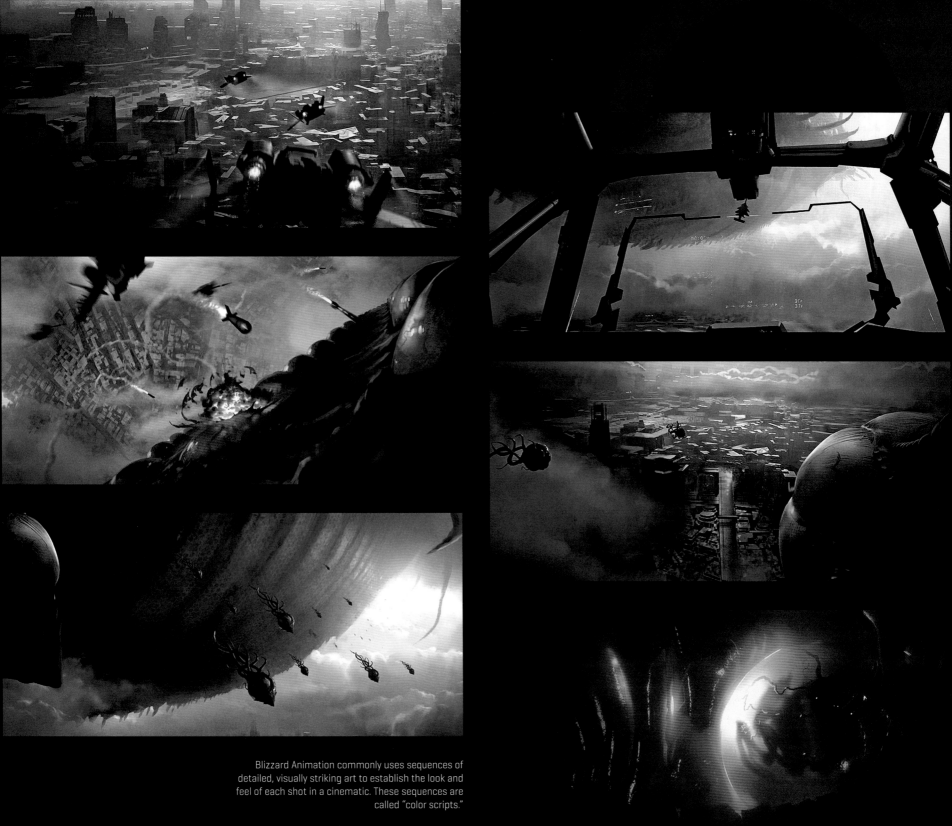

Blizzard Animation commonly uses sequences of detailed, visually striking art to establish the look and feel of each shot in a cinematic. These sequences are called "color scripts."

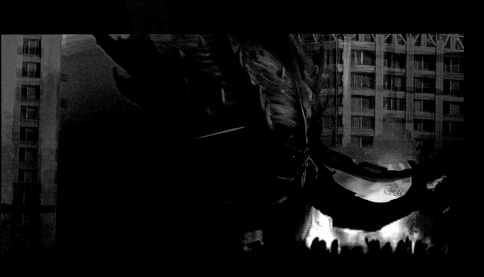

These color scripts help set a tone or establish contrast, such as the cool gray Korhal sky and the fiery explosions rippling across the screen.

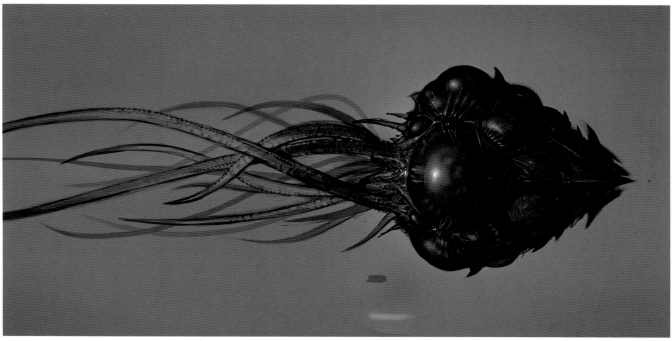

THE CINEMATIC ART OF **STARCRAFT**

ABOVE
Concept art for the inside of the zerg leviathan as it prepares to launch its forces.

LEFT
The exterior of a zerg drop pod.

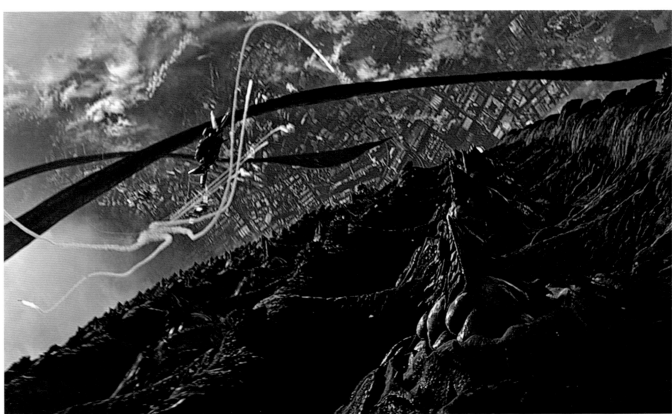

ABOVE
A modern sedan helps illustrate the scale of a drop pod.

RIGHT
A final still of the exterior of the leviathan just before a volley of missiles strikes.

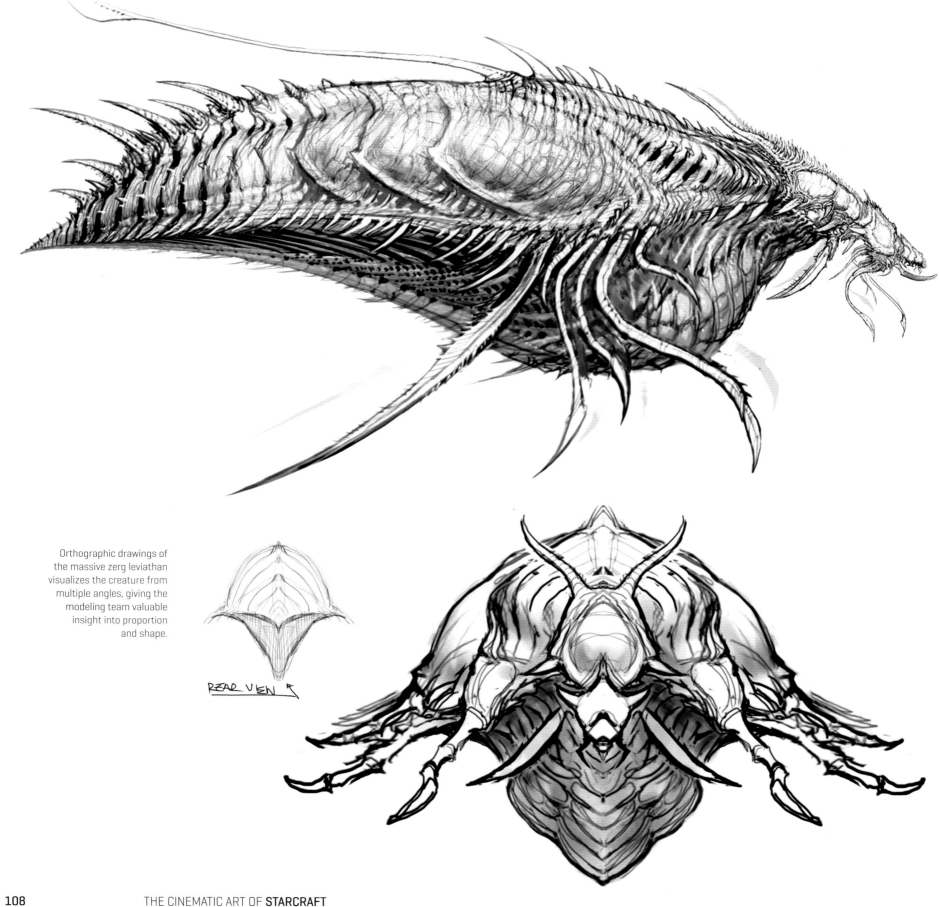

Orthographic drawings of the massive zerg leviathan visualizes the creature from multiple angles, giving the modeling team valuable insight into proportion and shape.

REAR VIEW

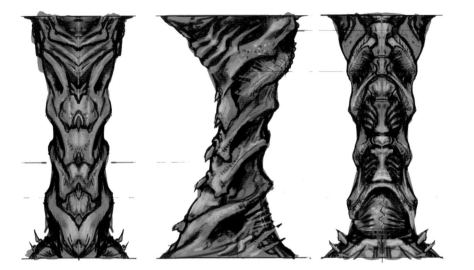

Concept art of the interior of the leviathan where Kerrigan plans her missions.

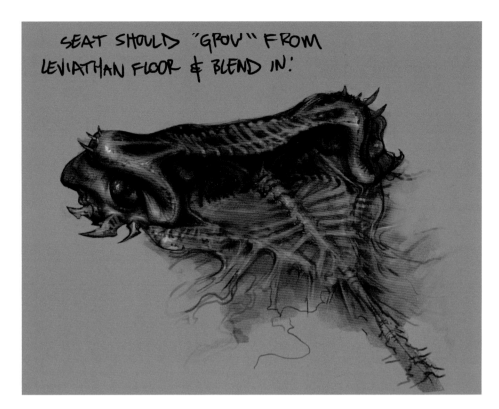

SEAT SHOULD "GROW" FROM LEVIATHAN FLOOR & BLEND IN!

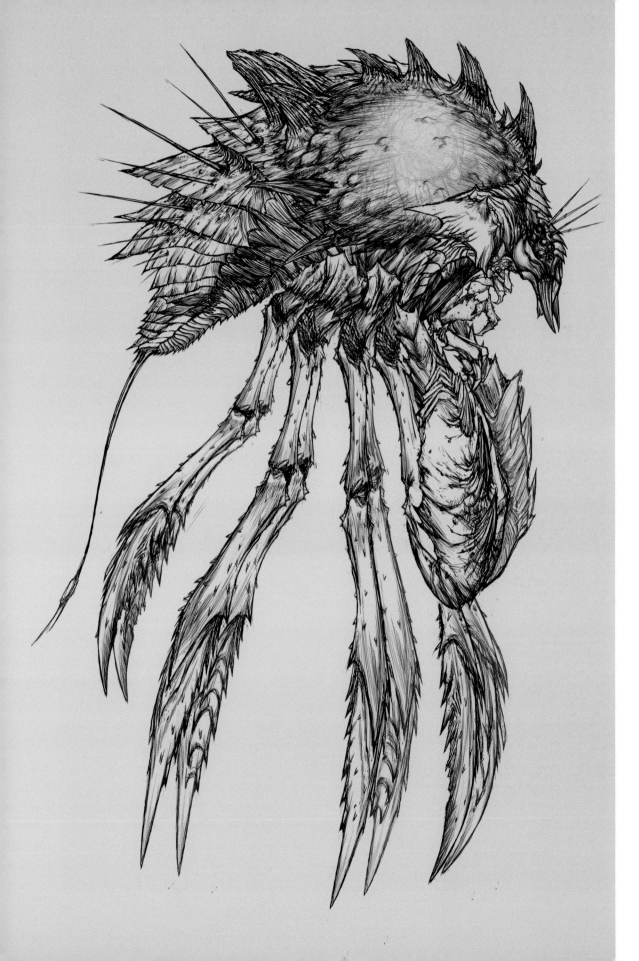

Concept sketches and art
for a zerg overlord.

LEFT AND MIDDLE
Concept art of a nydus worm
bursting out of the ground.

FAR RIGHT
The final 3-D model.

MANY *STARCRAFT* CINEMATICS HAD DEPICTED action sequences. Very few had shown the kind of extended, full-blown battles that players often experienced in-game. Even casual players knew the glory of directing their massive army to crash into another, the awe of watching destruction rain down on the battlefield, and the desperation of trying to position their units to take advantage of the chaos.

Kerrigan's assault against Arcturus Mengsk and the world of Korhal played out like a grandmaster zerg player taking on a newbie terran commander: marines ripped apart by strategically placed drops, armored ultralisks shrugging off volleys of siege tank fire, packs of zerglings and banelings darting through the explosions to surround the overmatched humans, and the defensive lines of the terrans bypassed entirely by the well-timed emergence of a nydus worm.

It was an extreme expression of the zerg's might. But at the beginning of *Heart of the Swarm* it was unclear whether Kerrigan would ever see it come to pass . . .

ABOVE
Untextured 3-D model of a
terran tank in siege mode.
Assets like this are called
"clay renders" because of
their gray, uncolored look.

ABOVE AND RIGHT
Concept art and the final
3-D model of a viking in
ground-assault mode.

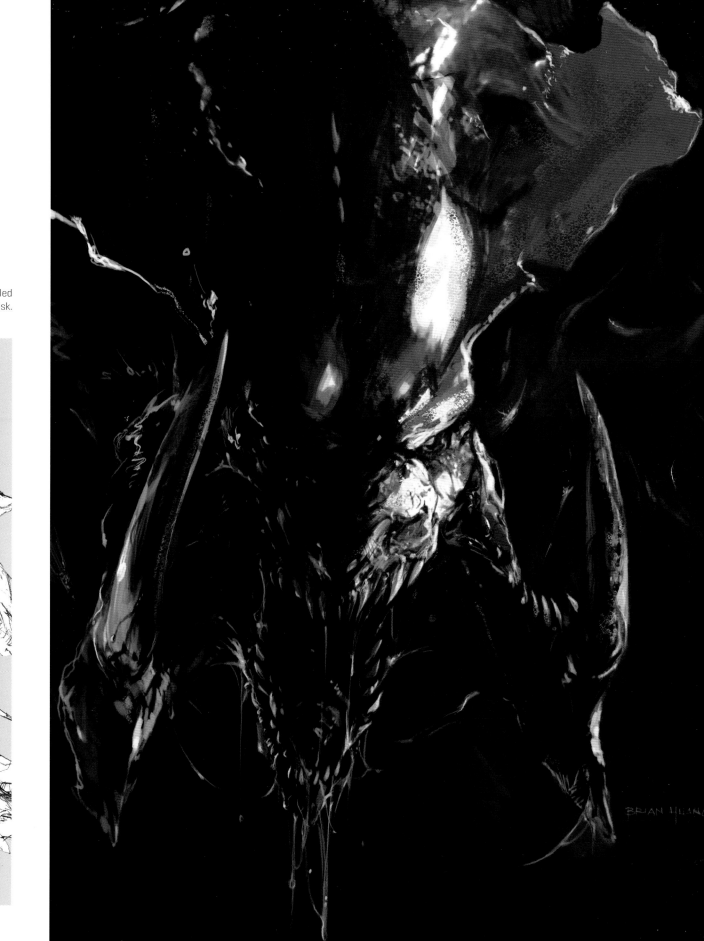

A sketch and detailed concept art for a hydralisk.

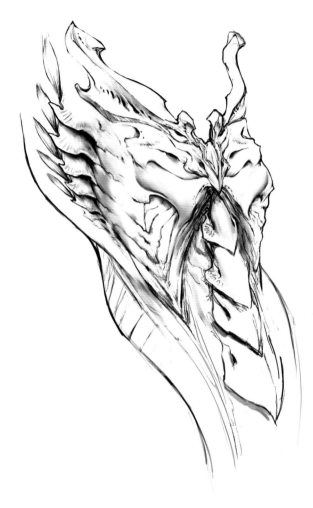

Concept illustration and detail sketches exploring a hydralisk's anatomy. Some sketches lack arms to allow modelers a full view of the torso.

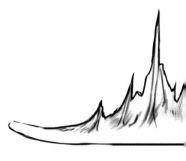

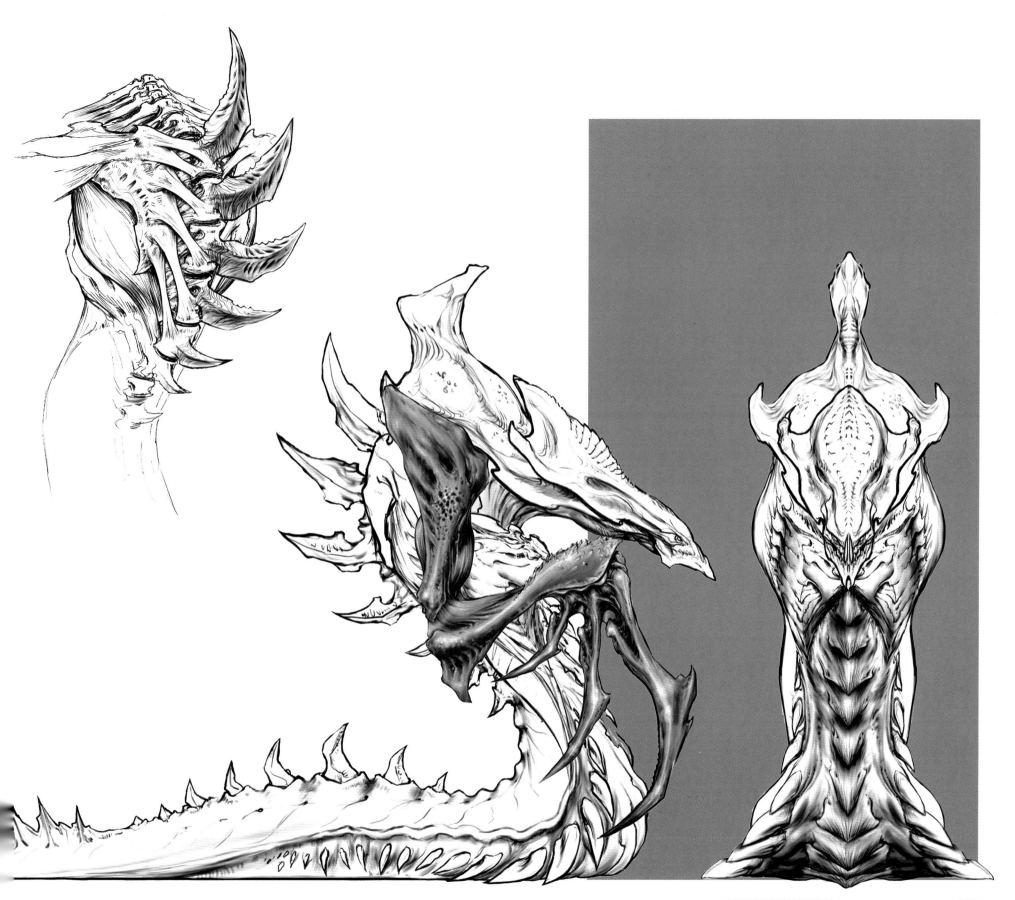

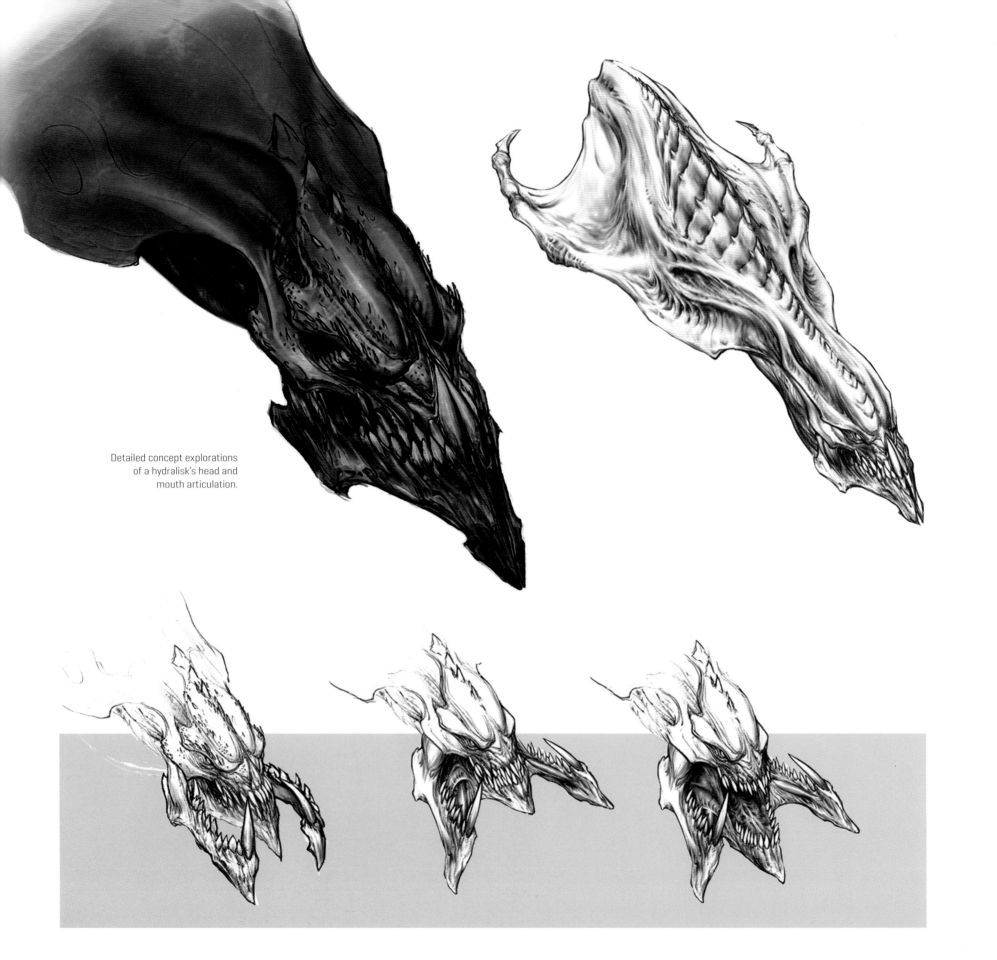

Detailed concept explorations of a hydralisk's head and mouth articulation.

The full 3-D model of the hydralisk is fairly long. These renders fully realize the alien's anatomy.

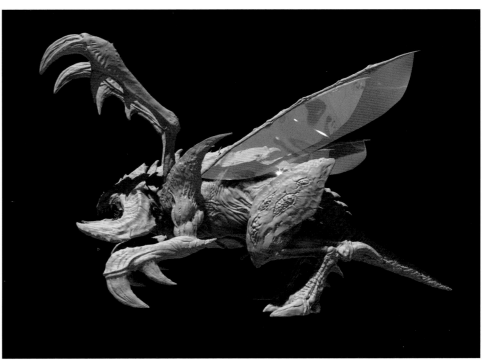

The zergling's journey from concept to final model requires significant attention to detail, especially to make its skin look believable and to make its translucent wings reflect and refract light properly.

The 3-D model of a baneling tucked into its centrifugal hooks and preparing to roll. The sac of corrosive bile was shaded and textured to give the appearance of glowing from within.

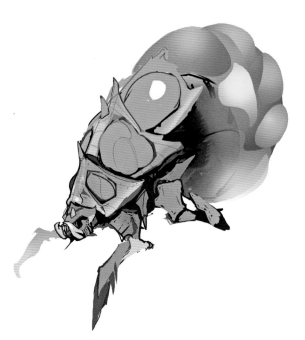

Clay renders and the full textured
model of the massive ultralisk.

Concept paintings and sketches of the streets on Korhal.

Concept art showing the scale of Korhal's buildings from a ground perspective.

that had dozens of zerg scurrying around the screen simultaneously. There were even a few that showed hundreds.

It wasn't possible to animate the movements of each creature manually, not if the cinematics team wanted to finish the project on time. Luckily, most of the Swarm were performing the same action for the whole cinematic: sprinting headlong into terran defenses.

Animators created looping cycles of the creatures running and used basic behavioral systems to keep them together as they raced toward their terran enemies. These systems allowed cinematic artists to simply point the zerg in the right direction and let them off their leashes, which was useful in the wide shots where the audience could only see the sheer breadth of the battlefield.

THE SCOPE OF THIS CINEMATIC WAS EXTREME.
Not only did the camera rest at ground level, showing the towering skyscrapers of Korhal up close, it also showed the battle from the sky which let the audience see for miles in each direction as the Swarm descended. Units would sometimes swoop inches past the camera even as dozens more bombarded the background.

The stormy skies and the distant cityscapes were mostly achieved with matte paintings—hyper-realistic illustrations that seamlessly connected a distant landscape to the modeled sets.

However, the cinematics team rarely had the luxury of simply setting them in the background. In most action scenes, the camera moved extensively along three axes. The different planes of the matte painting— skyscrapers in the midground, a crashing battlecruiser in the background, and the sky even further in the background—had to be tracked separately in 3-D space, a task that required precise work.

It was a huge amount of effort for something that had to be completely invisible to the audience.

Many concepts of Korhal were needed before the final shot (upper right) could be completed. The concept of Korhal at sunset (bottom) was too peaceful for the opening cinematic but helped inform the look of the final shots of the campaign.

Many of Blizzard's cinematics live beyond their original format. Certain iconic frames are re-rendered at a higher resolution without certain effects (like motion blur), then retouched for clarity and impact. These "paintovers" are frequently used for marketing or community purposes, such as releasing desktop wallpapers.

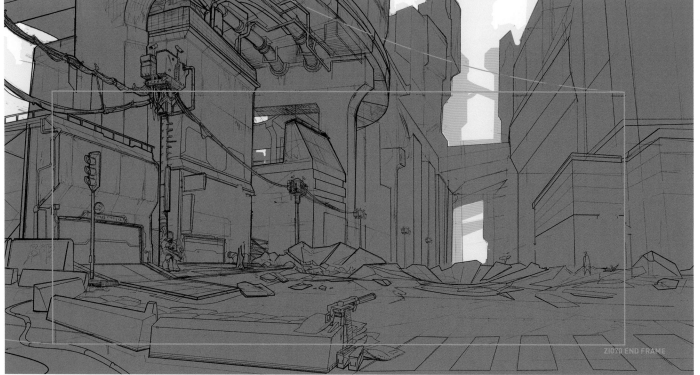

ABOVE
Color concept art of Korhal for the final cinematic of the campaign.

LEFT AND TOP RIGHT
Concept sketches with frame markers showing how zerg drop pods will land in the streets.

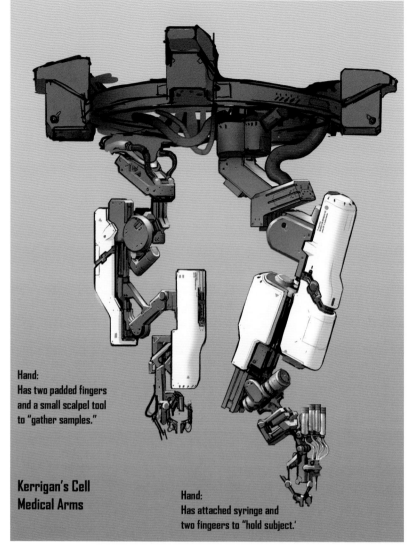

Hand:
Has two padded fingers
and a small scalpel tool
to "gather samples."

**Kerrigan's Cell
Medical Arms**

Hand:
Has attached syringe and
two fingeers to "hold subject.'

LEFT
Concept designs of Kerrigan's cell
in the Umojan laboratory.

Kerrigan's Cell
Bed Only

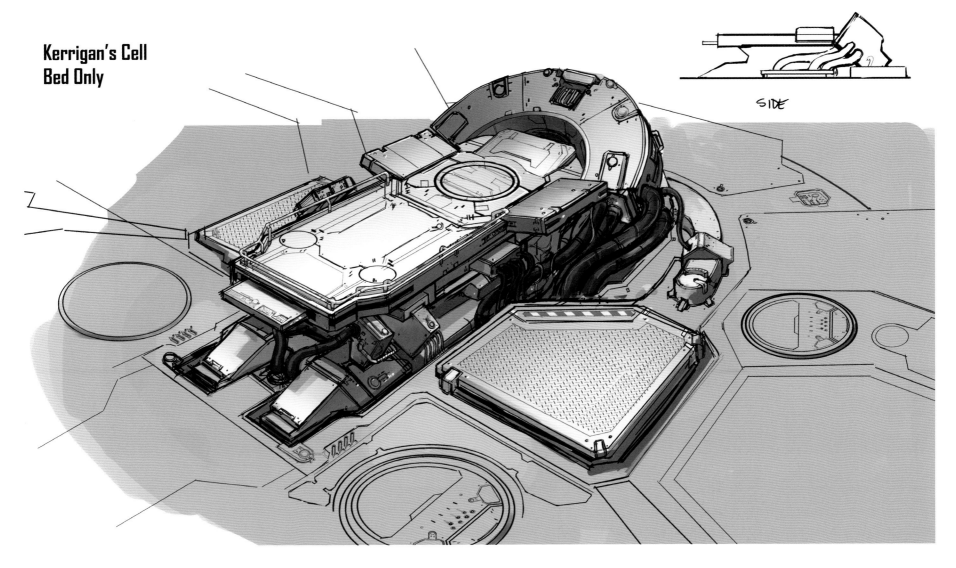

SIDE

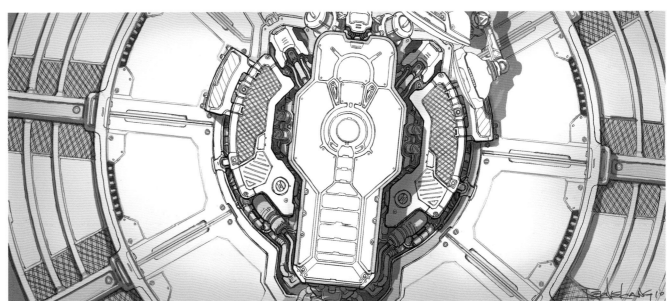

Only Kerrigan's bed can be seen in the opening of the zerg campaign. The rest of the environment is for in-game cinematics.

PROFILE WITH
VIEWING PLATFORM

Concepts for the Umojan laboratory
went through many iterations ranging
from test tubes to enclosed walls to
force field spheres.

All the designs focus on the idea that the terrans still fear Kerrigan and want to isolate her power.

Lab equipment designs try to
highlight the more advanced
technology of the Umojans.

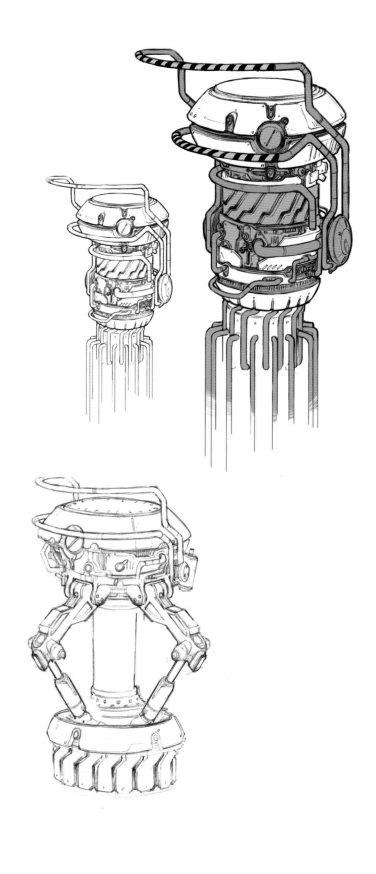

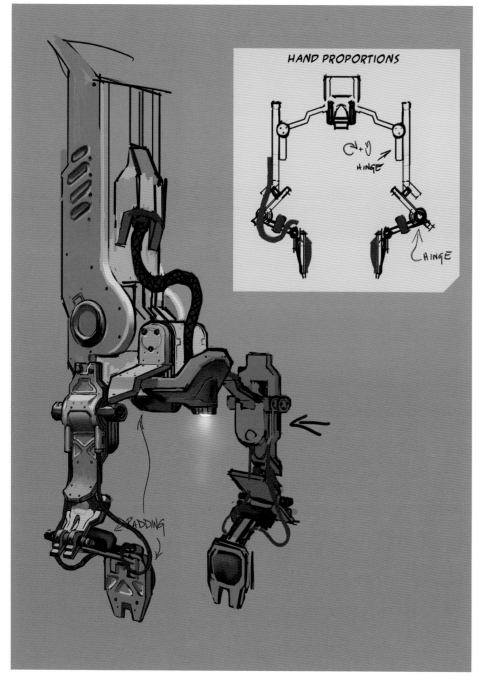

HAND PROPORTIONS

HINGE

HINGE

PADDING

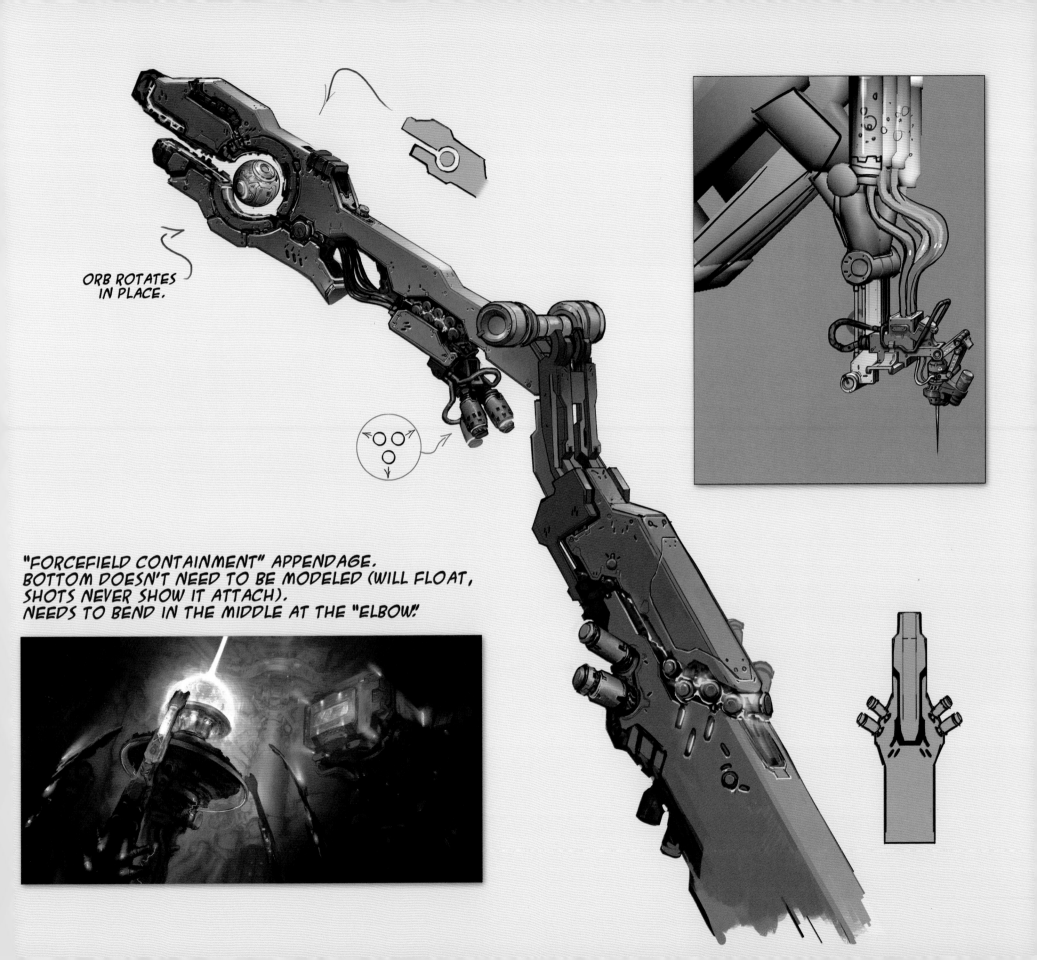

ORB ROTATES
IN PLACE.

"FORCEFIELD CONTAINMENT" APPENDAGE.
BOTTOM DOESN'T NEED TO BE MODELED (WILL FLOAT,
SHOTS NEVER SHOW IT ATTACH).
NEEDS TO BEND IN THE MIDDLE AT THE "ELBOW."

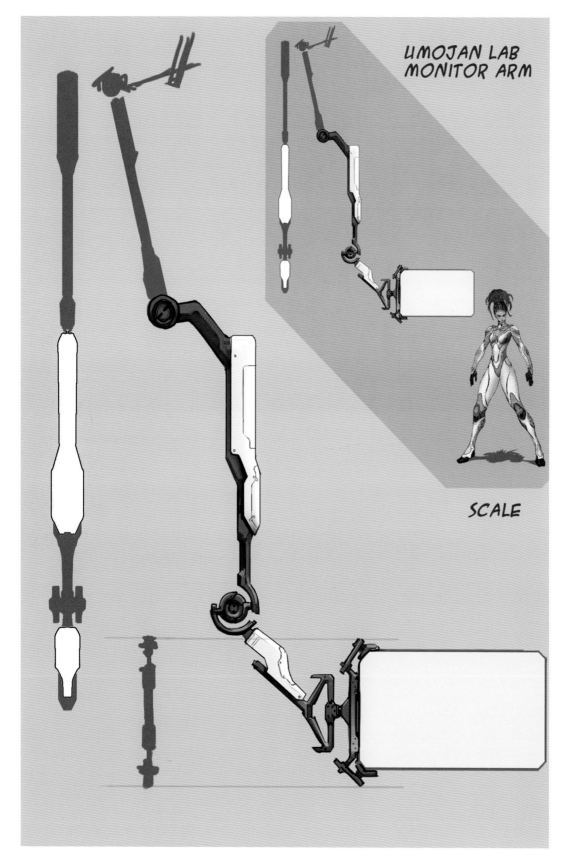

UMOJAN LAB
MONITOR ARM

SCALE

ABOVE
Color scripts for the first
in-game cinematic of
the campaign—Kerrigan
prepares for her final test
in the Umojan lab.

LEFT
Lab equipment details and
size comparison.

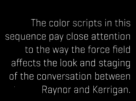

The color scripts in this sequence pay close attention to the way the force field affects the look and staging of the conversation between Raynor and Kerrigan.

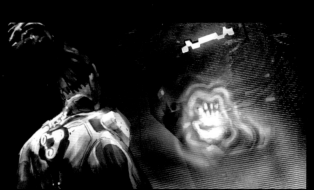

FORCEFIELD AND "TOUCH" FX

"IMPACT" STUDY

STATIC FORCEFIELD (IDLE)

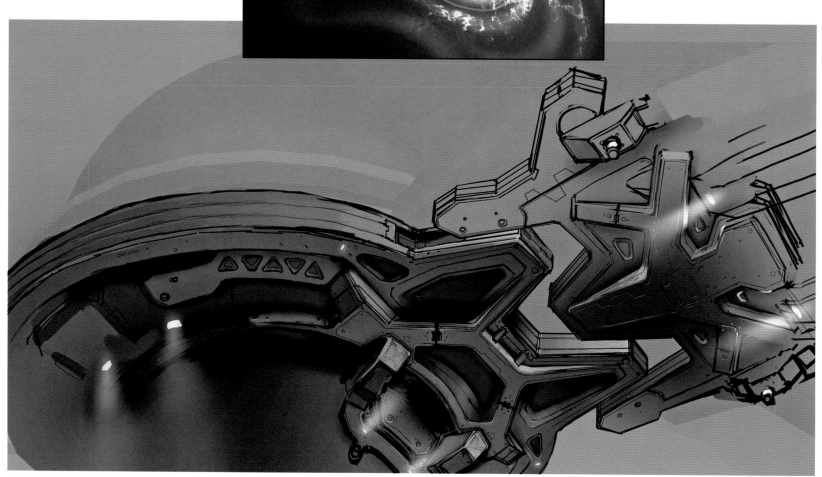

ABOVE
Effects studies for the force field on Kerrigan's cell.

LEFT
The underside of Kerrigan's cell and the mechanism by which the bridge attaches to it needed special attention from designers.

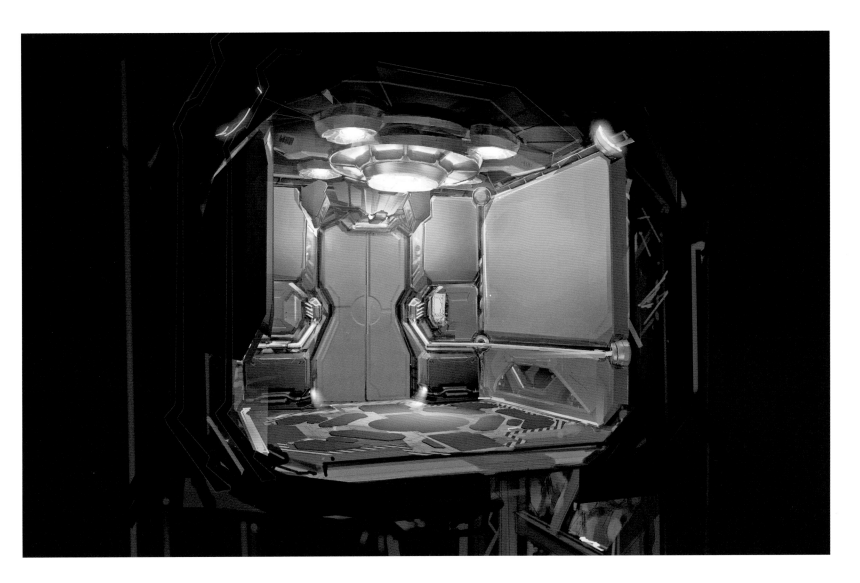

RIGHT
Concept illustration of the giant elevator in the Umojan lab.

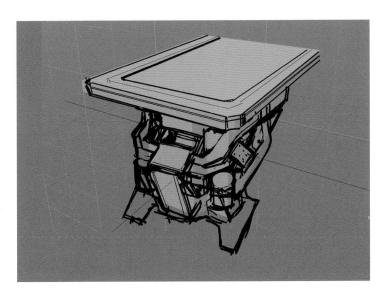

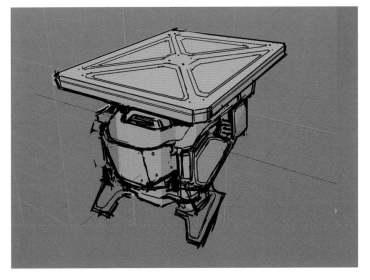

Line drawings exploring the elevator platform.

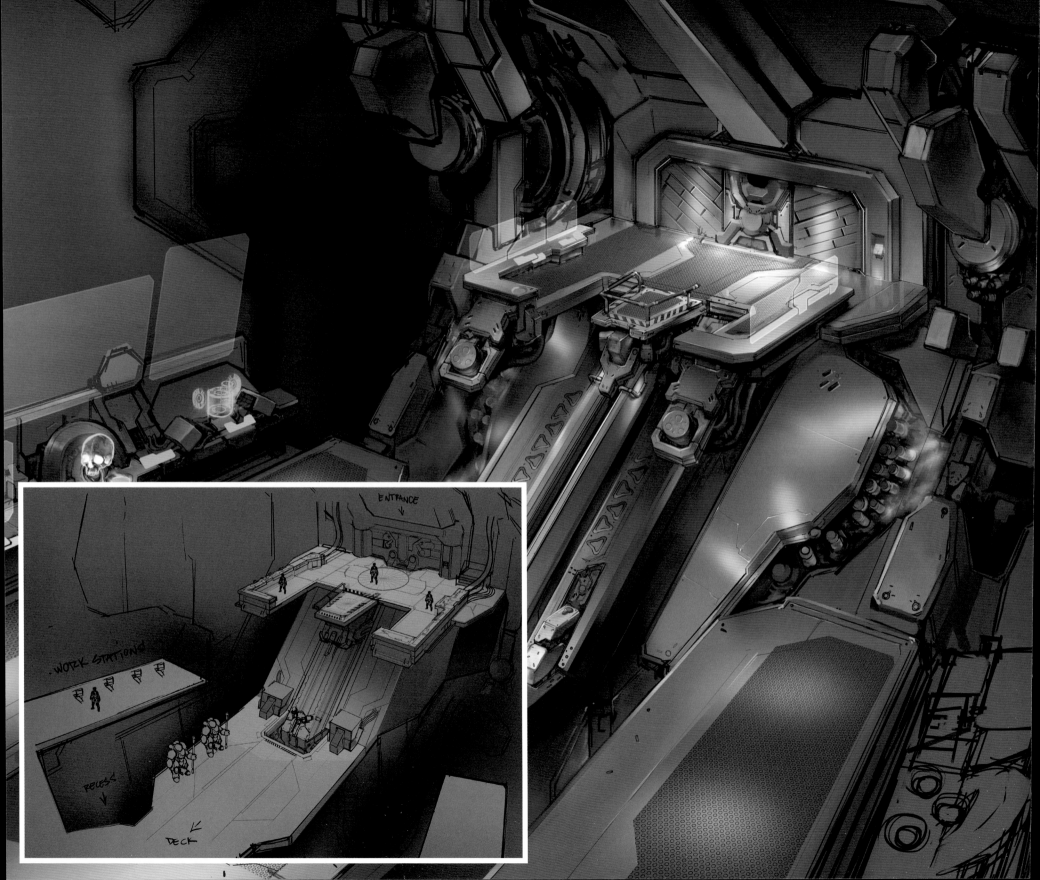

ENTRANCE

WORK STATIONS

RECESS

DECK

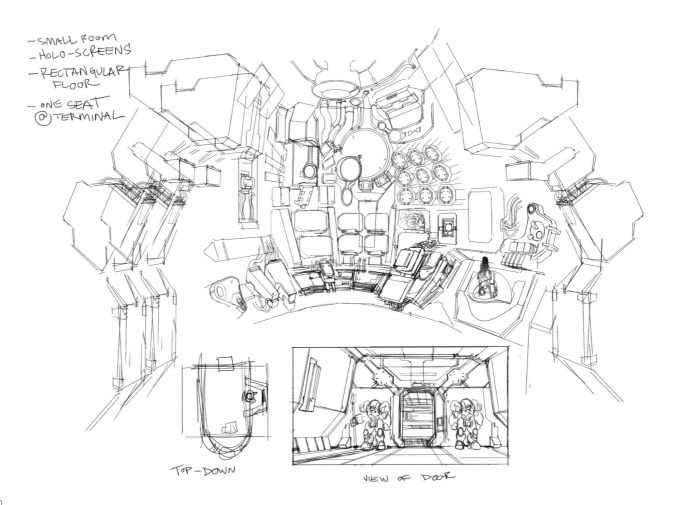

- SMALL ROOM
- HOLO-SCREENS
- RECTANGULAR FLOOR
- ONE SEAT @ TERMINAL

TOP-DOWN

VIEW OF DOOR

Raynor's entrance into the lab reveals a huge environment filled with advanced Umojan technology. Many details around the room, from the doors to the holograms, had considerable design iterations to find the right look.

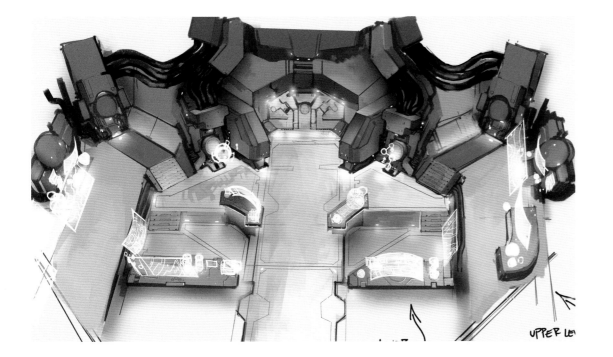

UPPER LEV

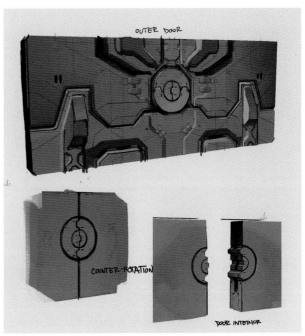

OUTER DOOR

COUNTER-ROTATION

DOOR INTERIOR

> "THE KILLING WILL
> NEVER STOP UNTIL
> MENGSK IS DEAD."
> —KERRIGAN

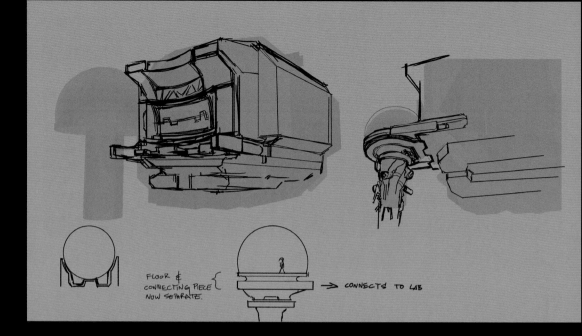

THE IN-GAME CINEMATICS IN *HEART OF THE Swarm* were significantly larger in scope than any of the ones in *Wings of Liberty*. From the first day of development, the cinematics team suspected that they would not be able to run these scenes in real-time. Their goal was to up the quality in every regard, which would have threatened to annihilate most computer systems for many reasons.

The secret Umojan research facility, built for several scenes at the beginning of the campaign, was a bigger set than almost every location from the previous game combined. A plethora of environments, textures, and characters—ranging from scientists to assassins to packs of primal zerg—created a memory footprint far beyond the RAM capacity of most computers. Advancements in the game engine's lighting and animation features were going to strain the CPUs and video cards of most players.

Doing all the cinematics in real-time was simply out of the question.

The optional character conversations onboard Kerrigan's flagship, the *Leviathan*, remained real-

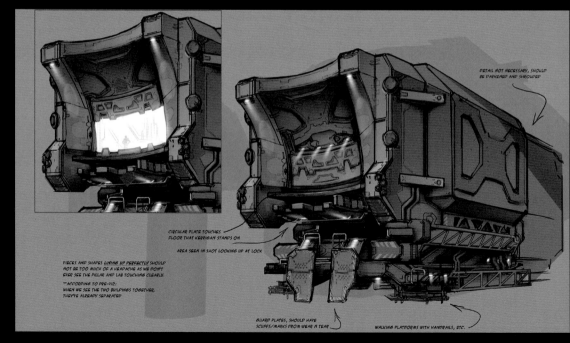

RIGHT
The Umojan facility sits on the edge of a large cliff. This concept art explores the shape of the whole building

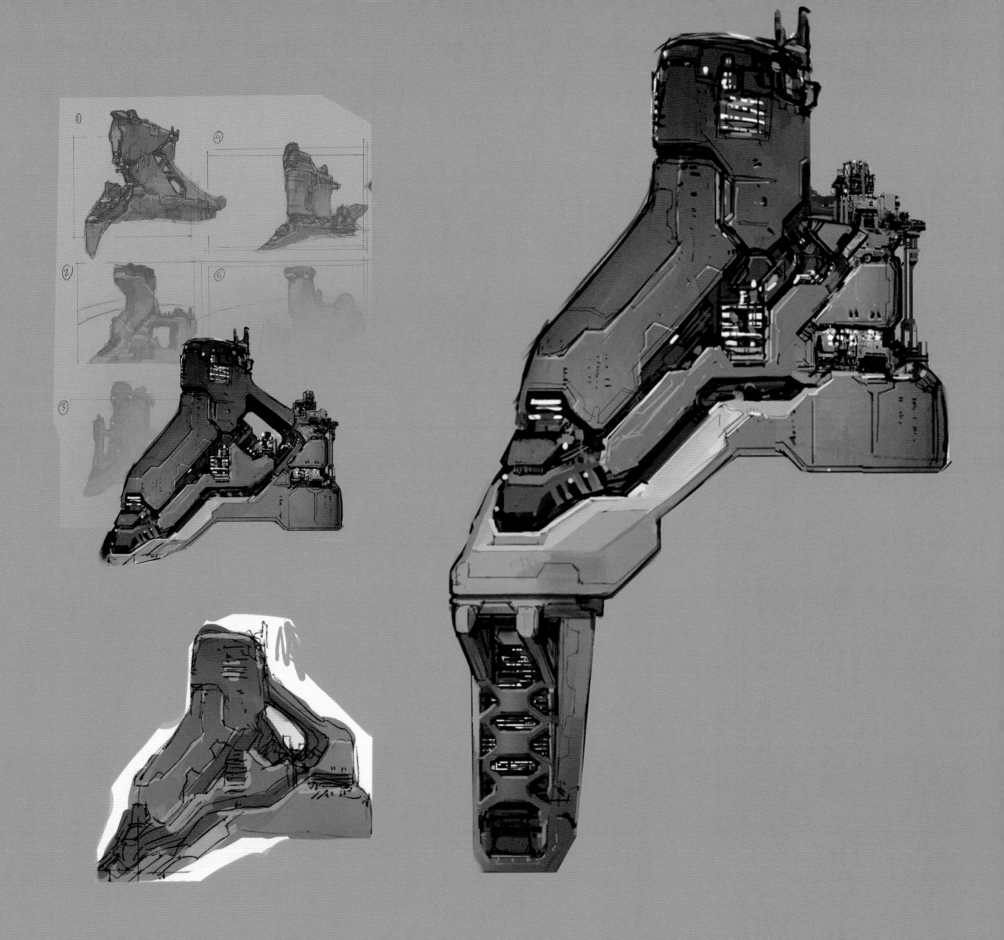

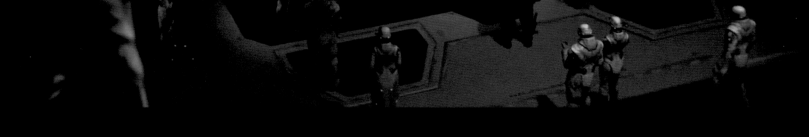

THE CINEMATIC ART OF **STARCRAFT**

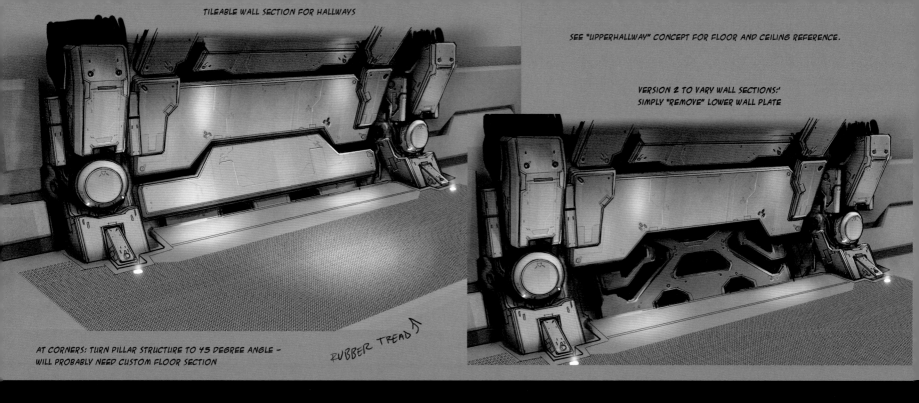

TILEABLE WALL SECTION FOR HALLWAYS

SEE "UPPERHALLWAY" CONCEPT FOR FLOOR AND CEILING REFERENCE.

VERSION 2 TO VARY WALL SECTIONS:
SIMPLY "REMOVE" LOWER WALL PLATE

AT CORNERS: TURN PILLAR STRUCTURE TO 45 DEGREE ANGLE –
WILL PROBABLY NEED CUSTOM FLOOR SECTION

RUBBER TREAD

THE LARGE SETS OF THE UMOJAN RESEARCH facility represented something *StarCraft* had never shown: the look of another human nation in the Koprulu Sector. It took multiple iterations of concept art and environmental design ideas before the team settled on an appropriate look.

The Umojan station was imagined as a particularly advanced facility that was filled with cutting-edge scientific research and highly-trained, orderly technicians. Not only did it immediately look different than the Dominion, but characters like Jim Raynor stuck out like a sore thumb, which made it clear why he was itching to leave.

The aesthetic applied to almost every human character in the facility, from the guards in pristine combat armor to the researchers carrying scientific instruments. Even the aesthetic of the facility doors and force-fields flowed into the look.

Of course, it didn't stay pretty and clean for long. This was the Koprulu sector. It was only a matter of time before war made a mess of things.

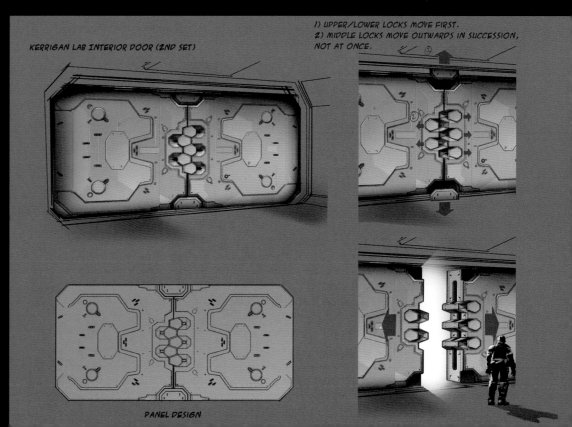

KERRIGAN LAB INTERIOR DOOR (2ND SET)

1) UPPER/LOWER LOCKS MOVE FIRST.
2) MIDDLE LOCKS MOVE OUTWARDS IN SUCCESSION, NOT AT ONCE.

PANEL DESIGN

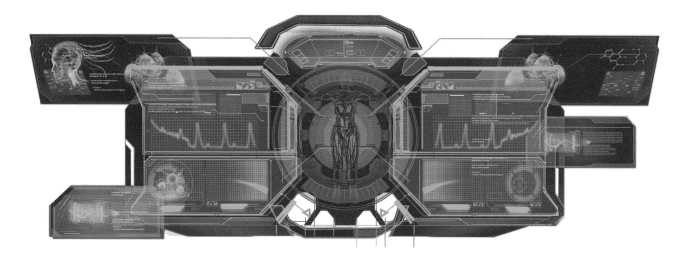

Concept art for the many holograms and scientists around the laboratory.

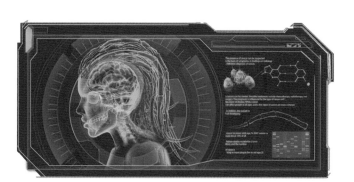

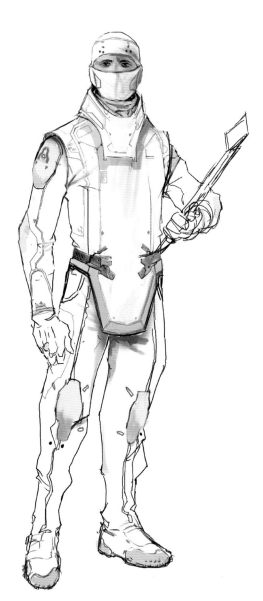

THE CINEMATIC ART OF **STARCRAFT**

The modularity makes it easier to create a crowd of "extras" in the scene by swapping around their heads, props and costume items.

HEAD PIECES
(MODULAR – MIX AND MATCH)
(60 ON BOTH SIDES)

?

HEAD #2
NO COLLAR
DIFFERENT CLOTH PATTERN
(TOP LAYER WRAPS AROUND EARS)

IMOGEN

DOMINION
DROP-POD

Concept iterations of a
marine drop-pod.

Drop pod concept art, including
specific size comparisons and a
demonstration of how it functions.

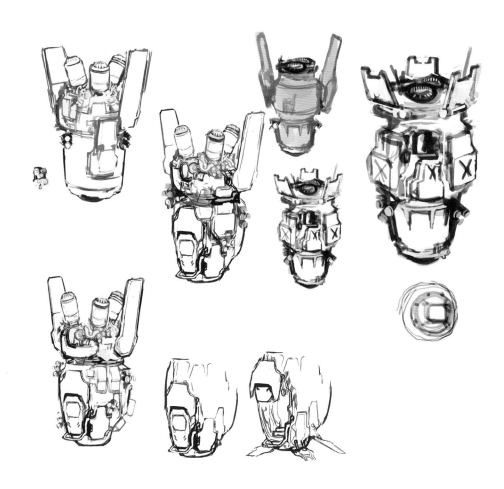

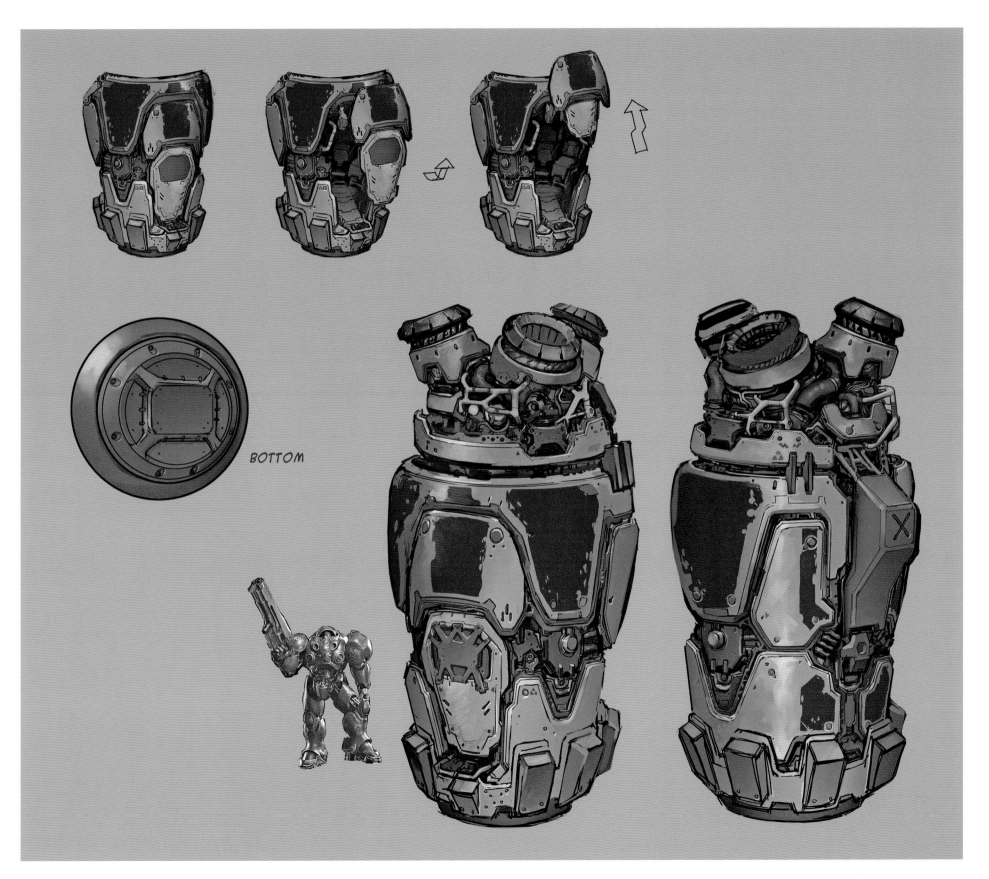

BOTTOM

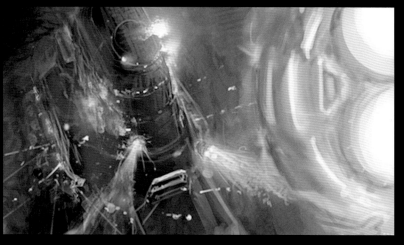

Color scripts for the Dominion assault
on the Umojan laboratory.

Color scripts are especially useful in determining
lighting needs and camera framing.

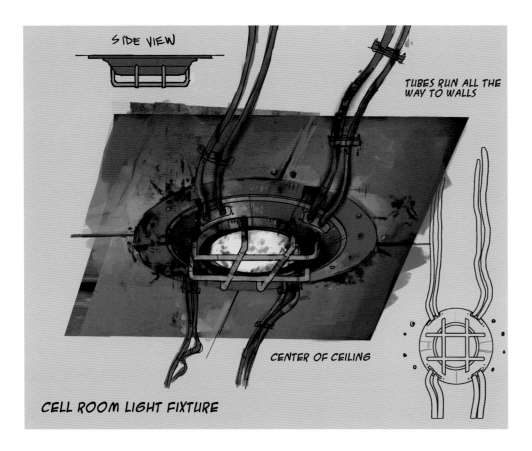

SIDE VIEW

TUBES RUN ALL THE
WAY TO WALLS

CENTER OF CEILING

CELL ROOM LIGHT FIXTURE

I.G.C.

JP WUZ HERE

Concept art of Raynor's cell, complete
with molding filth, bloodstains, and
an appropriate amount of easter eggs
scratched into the walls.

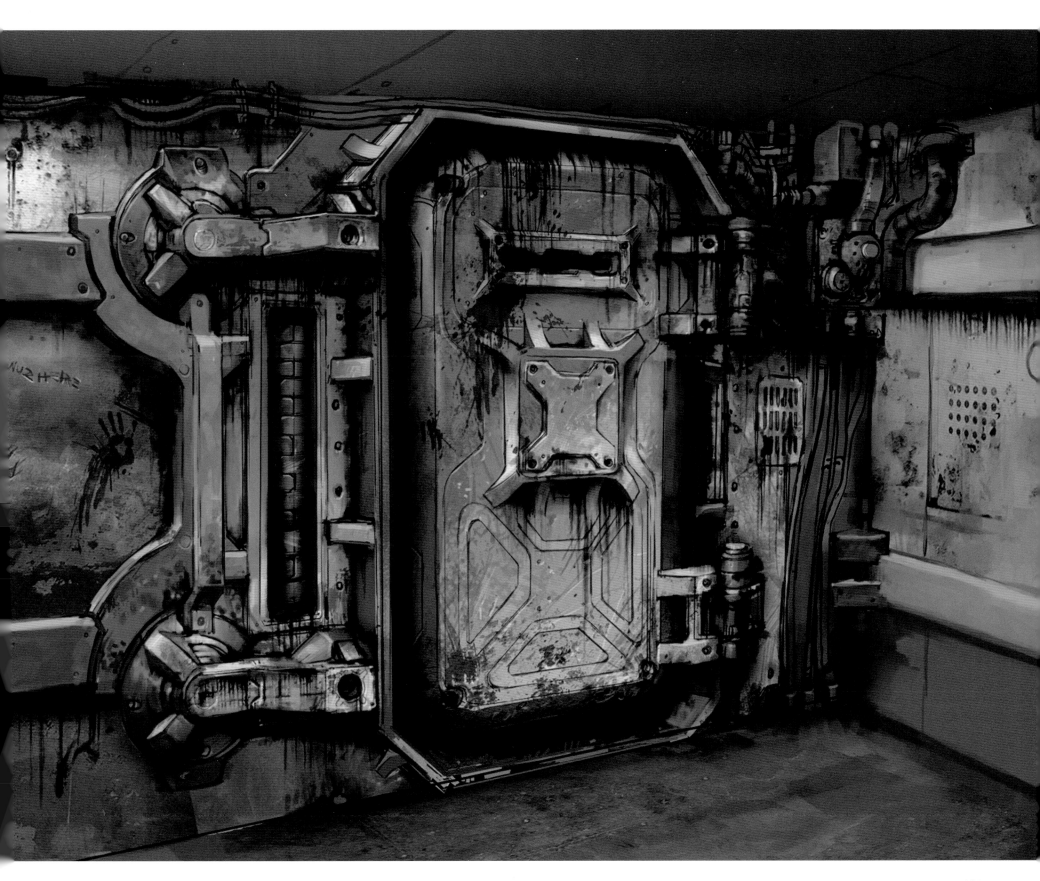

Concept art for Kerrigan's entrance to the xel'naga temple helps convey the massive scale of the environment.

The obelisks inside the temple are designed to look similar to the Keystone, since they are both constructs of xel'naga technology.

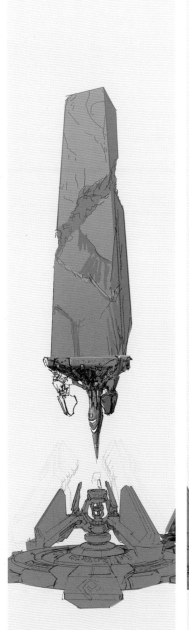

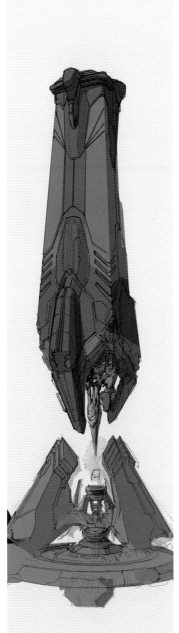
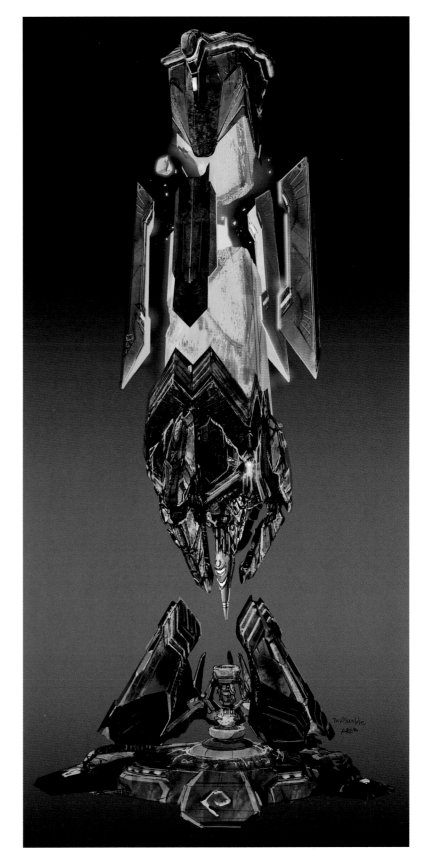

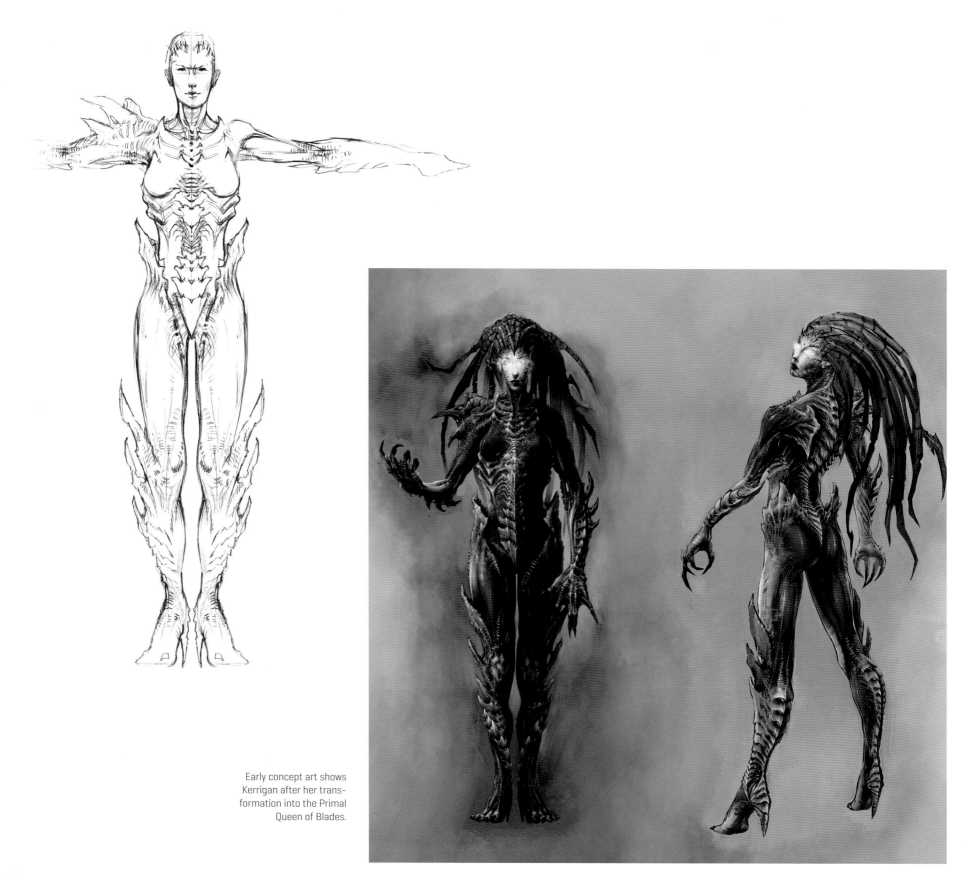

Early concept art shows Kerrigan after her transformation into the Primal Queen of Blades.

THE CINEMATIC ART OF **STARCRAFT**

Since the design process mainly focuses on what the camera sees, many iterations took place before the look of Kerrigan's natural "armored plating" felt right to the cinematics team.

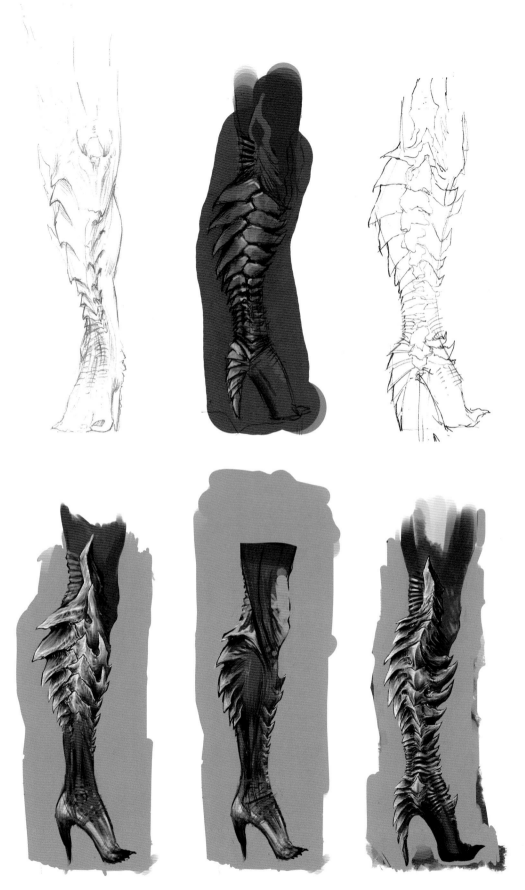

Very early concepts of Emil
Narud, one of Amon's most
powerful minions

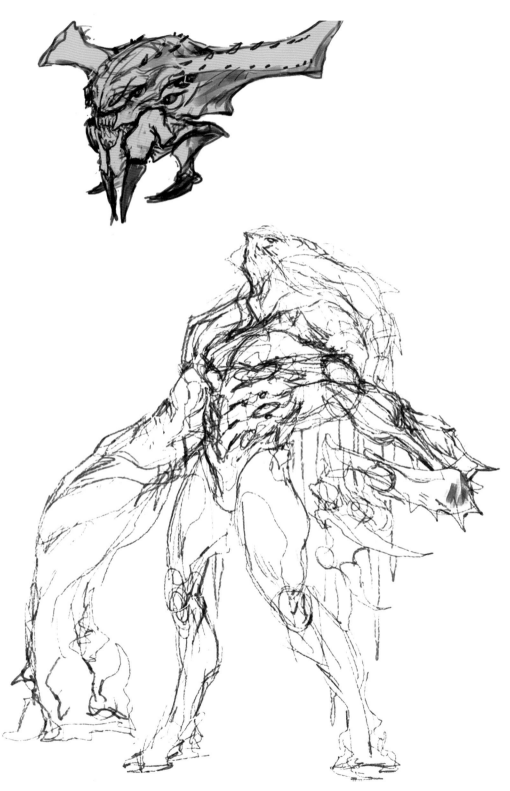

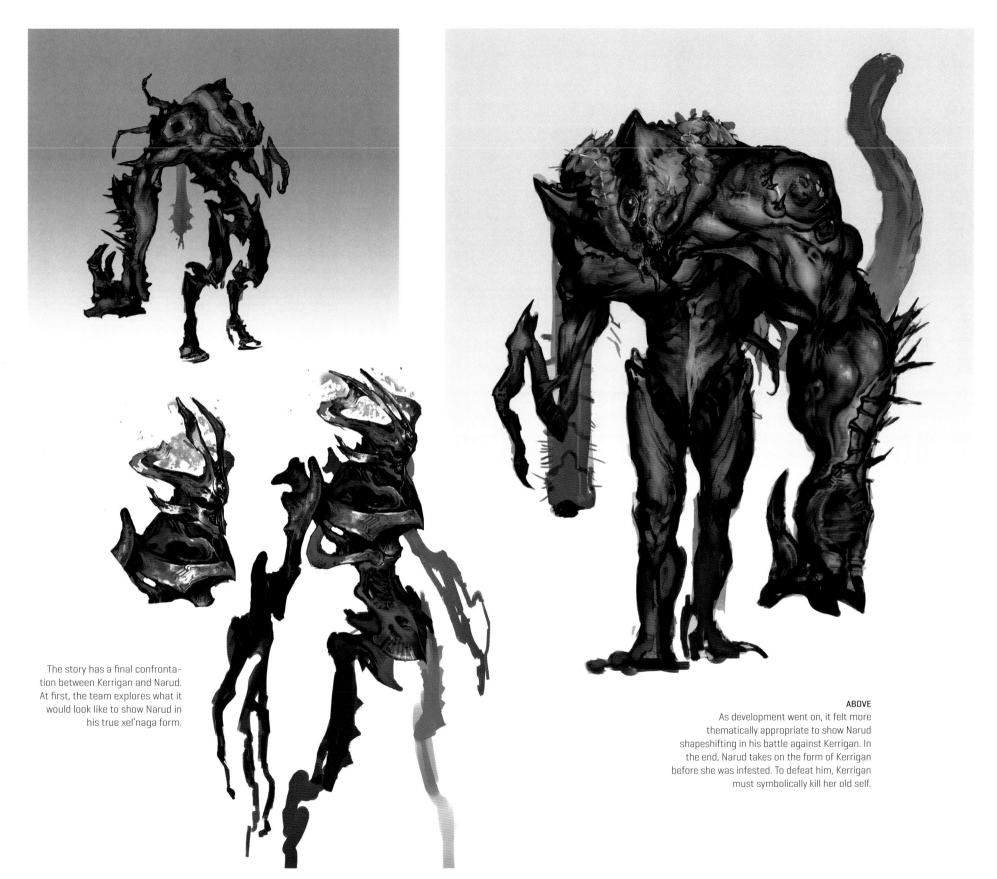

The story has a final confrontation between Kerrigan and Narud. At first, the team explores what it would look like to show Narud in his true xel'naga form.

ABOVE
As development went on, it felt more thematically appropriate to show Narud shapeshifting in his battle against Kerrigan. In the end, Narud takes on the form of Kerrigan before she was infested. To defeat him, Kerrigan must symbolically kill her old self.

For Kerrigan's transformation, concept artists explore whether her explosion of power striates vertically or in a spherical pattern. Each would have different implications for FX artists. The final cinematic uses the spherical pattern.

AT THE BEGINNING OF *HEART OF THE SWARM*, Sarah Kerrigan knew her path . . . she was a powerful psionic, a trained ghost assassin, and she still had some residual connection to the Swarm. She had one task in mind: kill Arcturus Mengsk. But committing to that path meant giving up Raynor. That was unthinkable.

Power, vulnerability, and rage were the aspects of Kerrigan that needed to be visible in her animations.

Overt displays of power counted for a lot—Kerrigan destroying a lab filled with enemy marines reminded the audience of how dangerous she truly was—but glowing pupils and exploding waves of psionic power could only carry so much.

In the first part of the campaign Kerrigan was heartbroken and furious upon hearing of Jim Raynor's execution. That emotion was fully visible in her eyes and came through in the subtleties of her facial performance.

Concept art of Kerrigan's cocoon on Zerus explores different shapes and sizes.

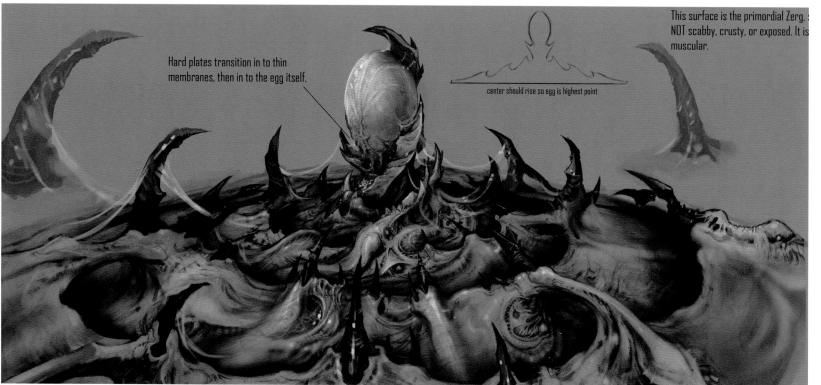

This surface is the primordial Zerg, NOT scabby, crusty, or exposed. It is muscular.

Hard plates transition in to thin membranes, then in to the egg itself.

center should rise so egg is highest point

More exploration of the organic "structure" surrounding the cocoon. Since this location is both in the game and the cinematic, shapes need to be clear and recognizable from both perspectives.

Both the landscape concepts and the designs for individual plants focus on making the world feel alien, primordial, and dangerous.

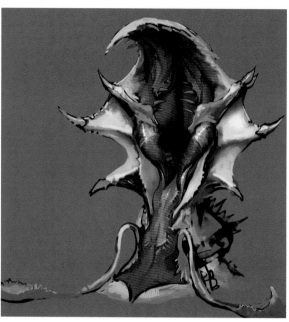

"HERE THE ZERG EVOLVED. AND HERE THE DARK ONE ALTERED THEM. THOSE LEFT BEHIND ARE THE PRIMAL ZERG."

—ZERATUL

ZERUS, THE ANCIENT HOMEWORLD OF THE zerg. A land where creatures hunted, killed, and evolved in a never-ending battle for dominance.

Cinematic artists created the look of the alien jungles from scratch. They made dozens of different models for the plant life and creatures that inhabited this hostile place. While many complex environments in *Heart of the Swarm* used matte paintings to fill out backgrounds, the entire scene on Zerus was fully rendered.

To get the look of sunlight filtering through a thick jungle canopy, lighting artists borrowed a technique from live-action filmmaking (known as using "cookies" or "gobos") to mock up the shape of long leaves waving in the breeze in front of the light source.

Showing the evolution of the primal zerg was a challenge that took some tinkering to get right. To show a creature gaining new eyes in a few seconds, animators and modelers created a single creature that had extra eyes hidden beneath the crags and folds of its rough hide. When the beast evolved into something larger, its hide "straightened out," revealing its previously unseen features. Audio design carried a lot of weight for this scene; the sound of cracking and straining bones created the illusion that an entire skeletal system was growing so quickly the creature was nearly pulling itself apart.

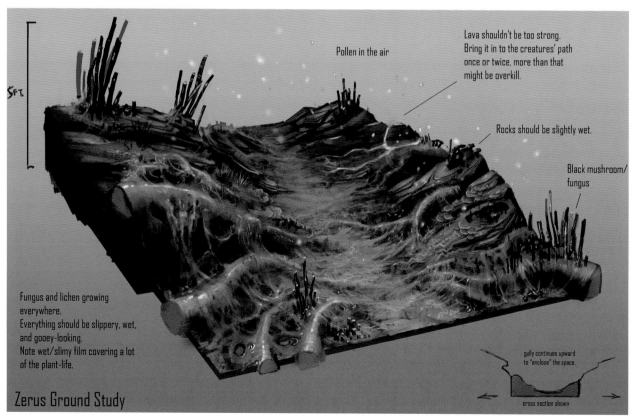

5 FT.

Pollen in the air

Lava shouldn't be too strong. Bring it in to the creatures' path once or twice, more than that might be overkill.

Rocks should be slightly wet.

Black mushroom/ fungus

Fungus and lichen growing everywhere.
Everything should be slippery, wet, and gooey-looking.
Note wet/slimy film covering a lot of the plant-life.

gully continues upward to "enclose" the space.

cross section shown

Zerus Ground Study

The introduction to Zerus shows this creature hunting down, killing, and consuming another animal . . . then evolving instantly.

Small Primal Zerg: Lion

POCKET FOR LARGE TOOTH

flesh near teeth/"lips" should be wet/red like human gums (high spec).

skin should be smooth when not scaled. OK to have areas with less detail. Underside should be smooth as well.

color pattern
- light tan on underside
- few bright orange stripes on throat and forehead.
- spikes/talons become tan/brown like exposed bone.

post-transformation
(has 3 eyes and spikes)

Big spikes grow during mutation

Yellow denotes exposed, dry shell/bone-like extrusions. Large plates should transition from skin to plates with small, dry scales that get bigger towards the protruded bone.

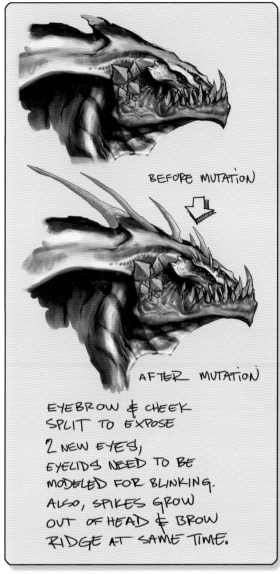

BEFORE MUTATION

AFTER MUTATION

EYEBROW & CHEEK SPLIT TO EXPOSE 2 NEW EYES, EYELIDS NEED TO BE MODELED FOR BLINKING. ALSO, SPIKES GROW OUT OF HEAD & BROW RIDGE AT SAME TIME.

This concept art explores how the transformation affects the creature's anatomy and head. In the final cinematic, the process is highlighted by showing the creature growing extra eyes.

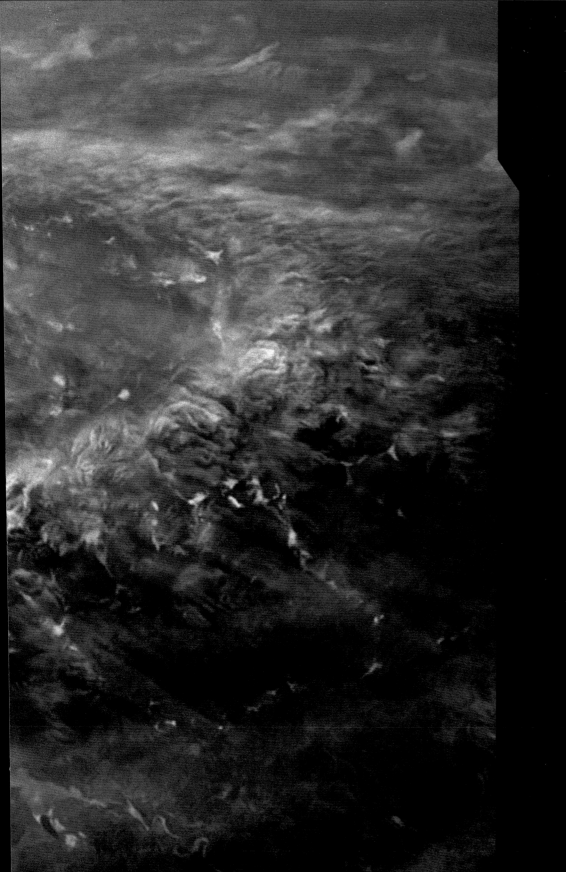

RETURNING SARAH KERRIGAN TO HER FULL glory as the Primal Queen of Blades required an avalanche of visual effects and lighting work. The scene began in stillness but ended with a hurricane of psionic power filling the atmosphere of Zerus while ranks of zerglings and hydralisks bowed to their queen.

"I was so afraid we would never get these shots to work! It felt like we could never get it perfect, and I still keep picking apart little details about it, but man . . . it looks so cool in context."

—SHIMON COHEN, VFX SUPERVISOR

These types of shots were wildly different than almost anything else in the *StarCraft* franchise. The scene opened inside Kerrigan's new chrysalis where she floated in a pool of liquid, which required cinematic artists to conjure up air bubbles in the fluid. The explosion of her newly-regained power first appeared as a column of light that stretched into the stratosphere then coalesced into a controlled sphere of pure energy that seemed ready to erupt in a lightning storm.

Many of the backgrounds—particularly the maelstrom in the sky and the shot of Zerus from orbit—relied heavily on matte paintings to portray the scale of this moment. Post-production compositing was used to bring all the environments, crackling power effects, and character models together in each shot.

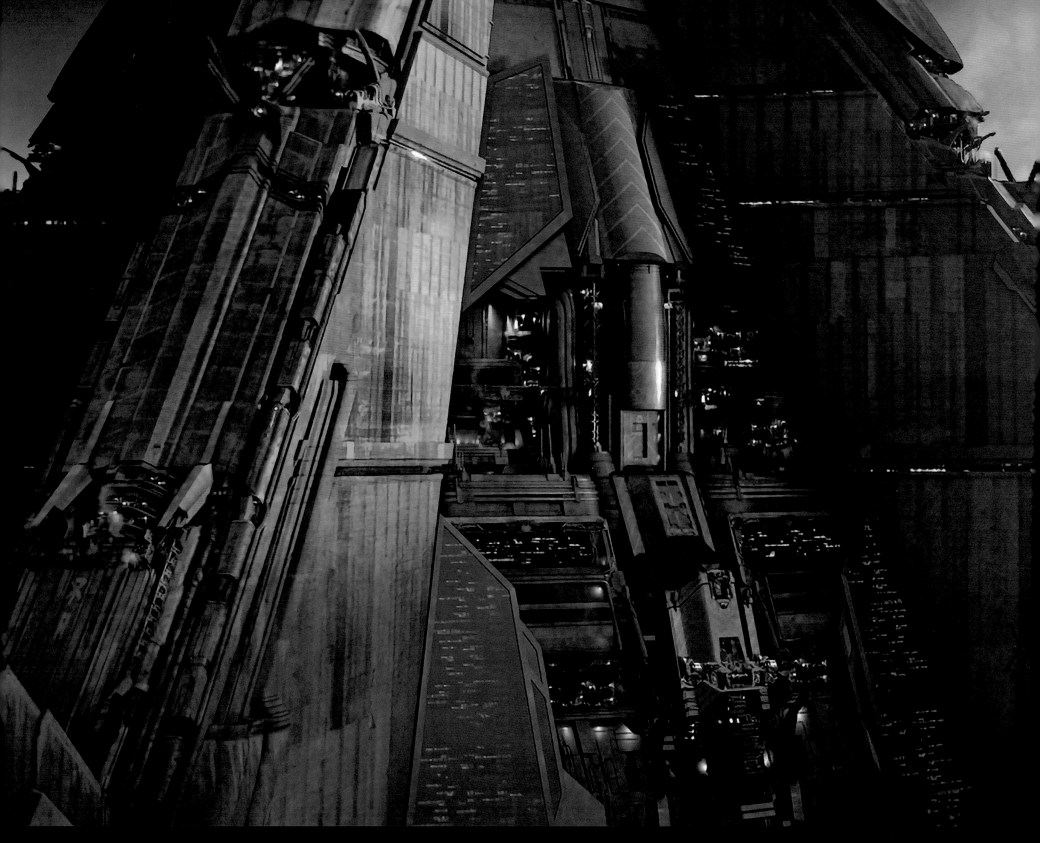

THE CINEMATIC ART OF **STARCRAFT**

The last cinematic in
Heart of the Swarm
depicts Kerrigan's assault on
Mengsk's stronghold. Before
she reaches the emperor,
she storms through his
considerable defenses.

NOW THAT THE IN-GAME CINEMATICS WERE being pre-captured, all the limitations that had existed in *Wings of Liberty* were gone. Action scenes no longer needed to be carefully situated in small locations with minimal amounts of characters.

Even so, the cinematics team was surprised at how massive some of *Heart of the Swarm*'s action beats would feel. When Kerrigan came face to face with a creature known as Narud, the fight escalated beyond anything ever shown in a Blizzard in-game cinematic. It resulted in a nydus worm bursting out of the ground to swallow Narud whole—a move that still doesn't end the fight. Between the apocalyptic brawl, the models of the corrupted doppelgangers who attack the Queen of Blades, and the extreme destruction of the set, it took months to complete the entire sequence.

Environmental destruction was tricky to show in-engine. The cinematic artists had to simulate the destruction of the floor and wall using external software tools. Once they captured the exact deformation of the terrain and the path of each piece of debris, it was all put back into the scene for final adjustment and rendering.

The brawl between Sarah Kerrigan and Zeratul, by contrast, did not have nearly the same level of pure destructive mayhem. However, the scene made up for it with Kerrigan's brutal hand-to-hand attacks that sent Zeratul flying across the set.

The physics of his clothing had to be simulated for each of his unscheduled trips across the cavern. These were tricky, time-intensive tasks that looked astonishingly real when pulled off.

Color scripts of Kerrigan's assault. The orange hue of the terrans' firepower contrasts heavily with the

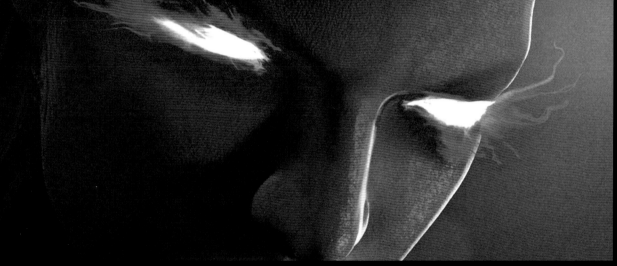

ELECTRIC
SPARKS

PARTICLES
CREATING
DEBRIS

Detailed concept art
shows different looks for
Kerrigan's devastating
attack on a viking.

MANY OF THE CAMERA MOVEMENTS IN *HEART
of the Swarm*'s action sequences were literally
created "by hand." Using a physical rig that recorded
movement, the director could adjust the POV as though
he were holding a live-action camera. Sometimes the
effect was used to create a sense of documentary
reality in the camera work, other times it was used
for long, ground-level orbits around characters in a
fight scene.

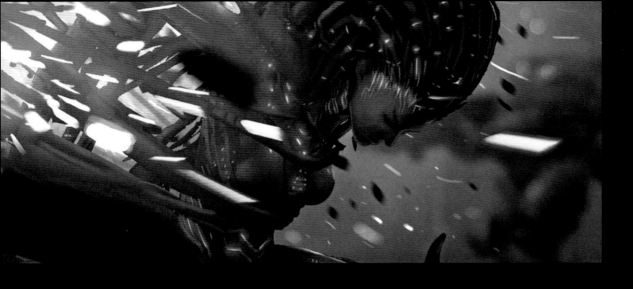

LEFT
Concept image focuses
on the colors and compo-
sition of Kerrigan bursting
through a viking.

BELOW
Detailed sketches inform
FX artists and modelers
how the vehicle should be
ripped apart.

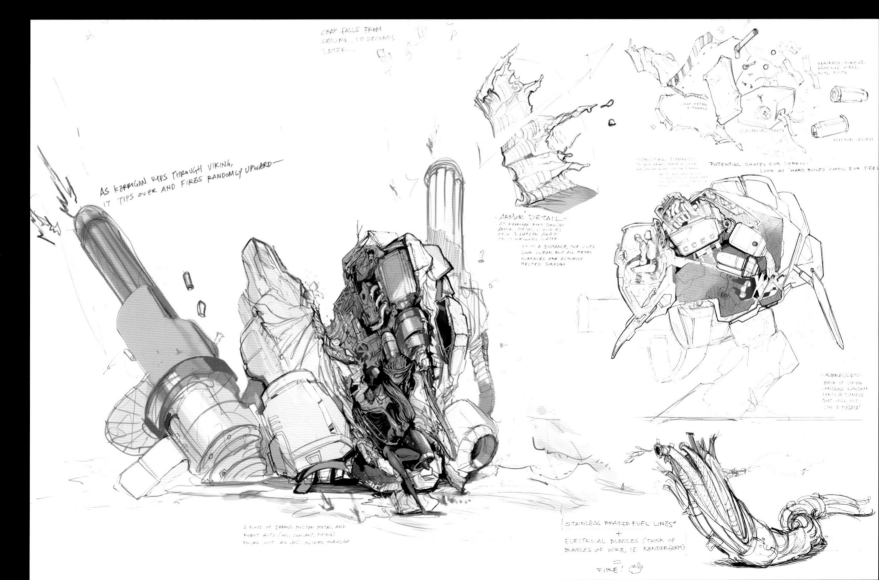

"...U CAN NEVER
...FER ENOUGH
...ALL THE LIVES
...'VE RUINED,
...TURUS."

...IGAN

A still image from the
final cinematic. Arcturus
Mengsk awaits Kerrigan in
the seat of his power.

Color scripts show the mood and feel of the confrontation between Mengsk and Kerrigan.

KA145

KA150

KA160

KA190

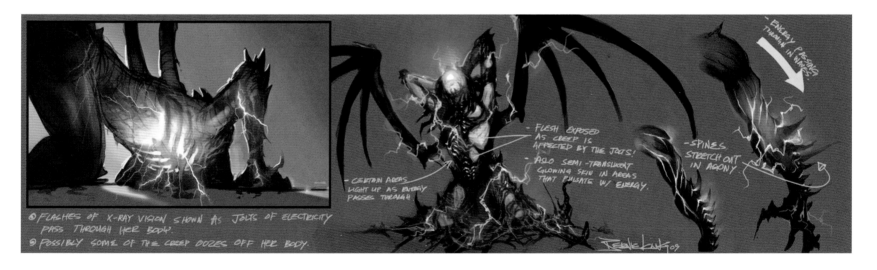

- ENERGY PASSING THROUGH IN WAVES

- FLESH EXPOSED AS CREEP IS AFFECTED BY THE JOLTS!

- ALSO SEMI-TRANSLUCENT GLOWING SKIN IN AREAS THAT PULSATE W/ ENERGY.

- SPINES STRETCH OUT IN AGONY.

- CERTAIN AREAS LIGHT UP AS ENERGY PASSES THROUGH

① FLASHES OF X-RAY VISION SHOWN AS JOLTS OF ELECTRICITY PASS THROUGH HER BODY.

② POSSIBLY SOME OF THE CREEP OOZES OFF HER BODY.

A concept sequence depicts Kerrigan
being incapacitated by the Keystone.
This is designed to inform FX artists
how the moment should look.

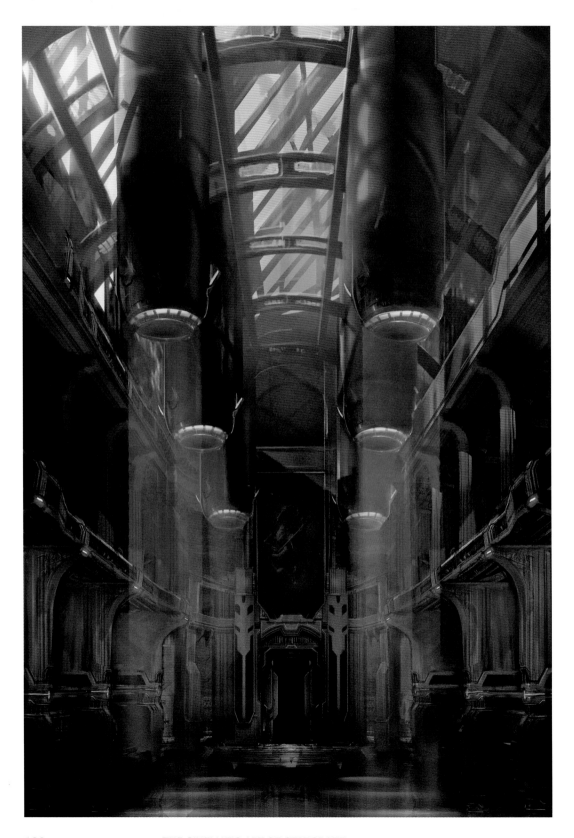

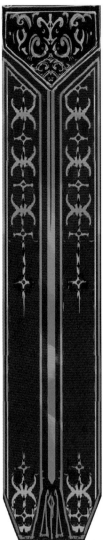

Concepts for Mengsk's quarters display the luxury he surrounds himself with during his time in power. From the gilded banners hanging from the ceiling to the elaborate window frames, his seat of power shows how he believes he deserves everything he has attained.

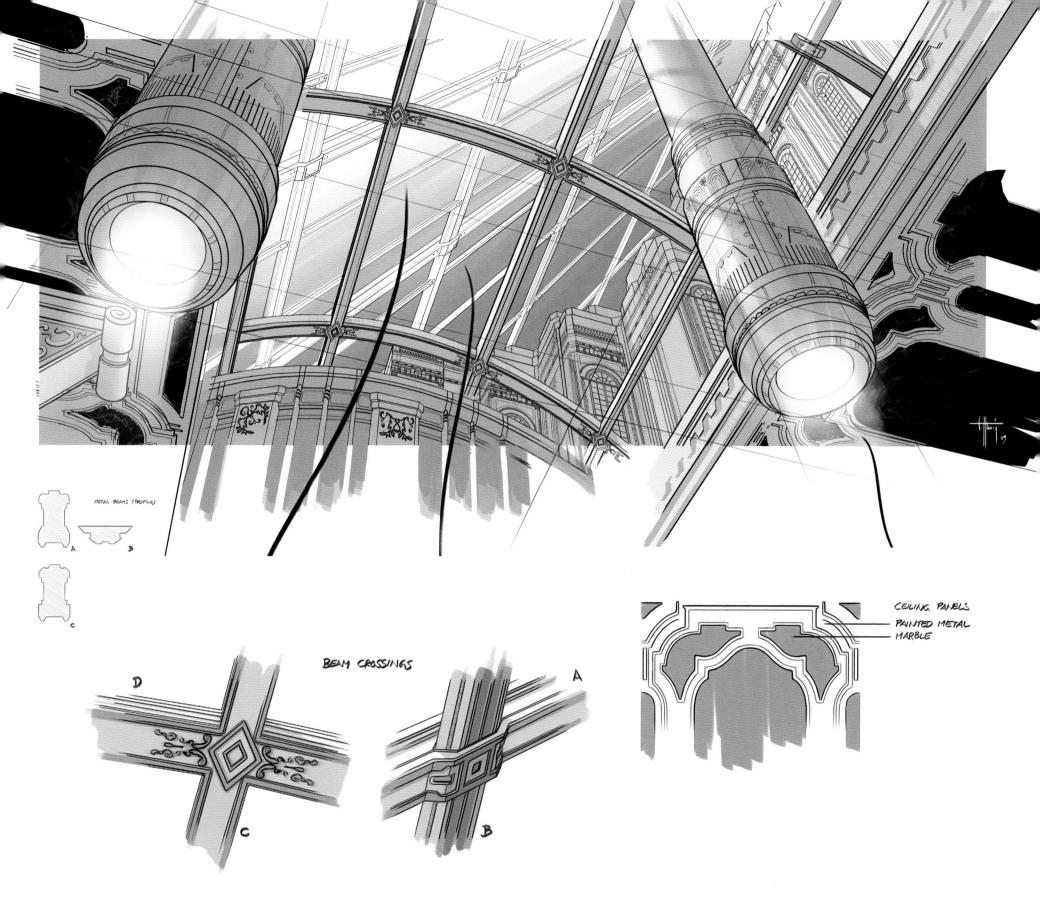

METAL BEAMS (PROFILE)

A
B

C

BEAM CROSSINGS

D

C

A

B

CEILING PANELS
PAINTED METAL
MARBLE

More concept art and design sketches show the architecture and accoutrements in the room.

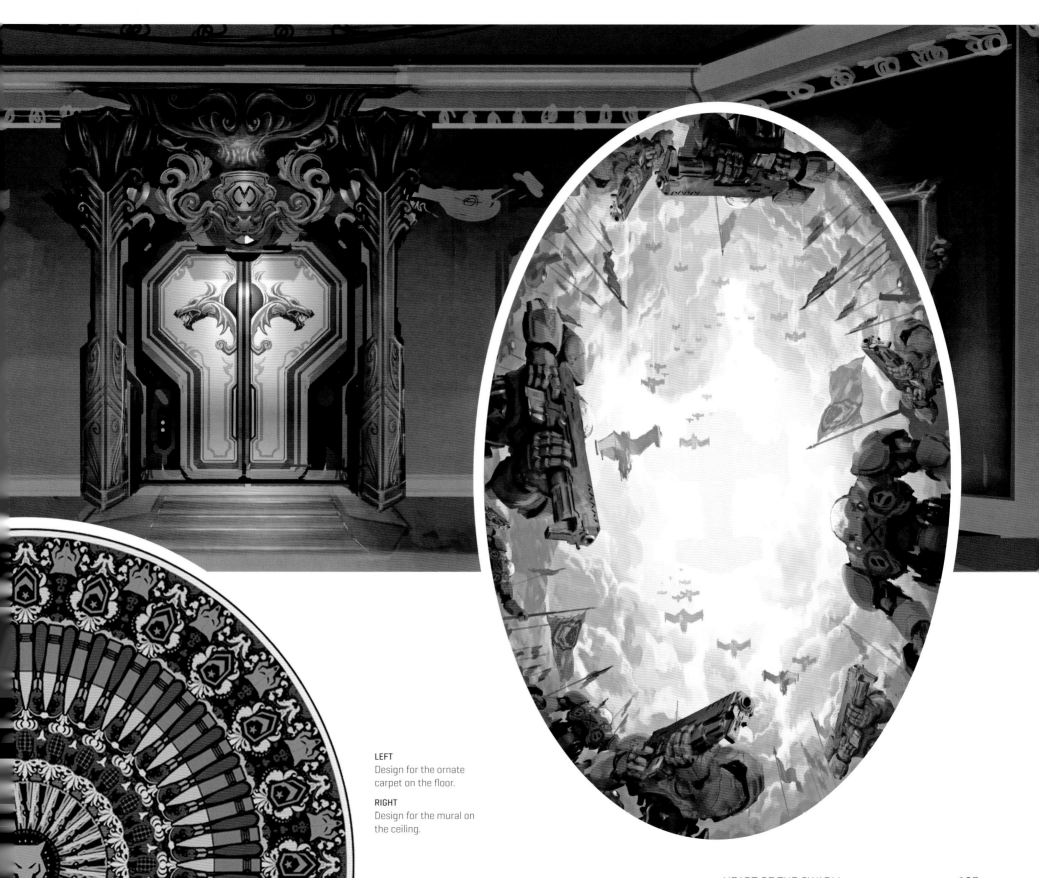

LEFT
Design for the ornate carpet on the floor.

RIGHT
Design for the mural on the ceiling.

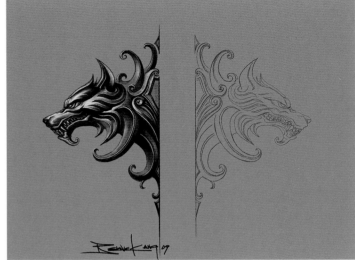

The design for the door mimics the sigils on Arcturus's clothes in earlier cinematics. In this case, his buckle (above, lower image) is embellished like the golden imagery on the door.

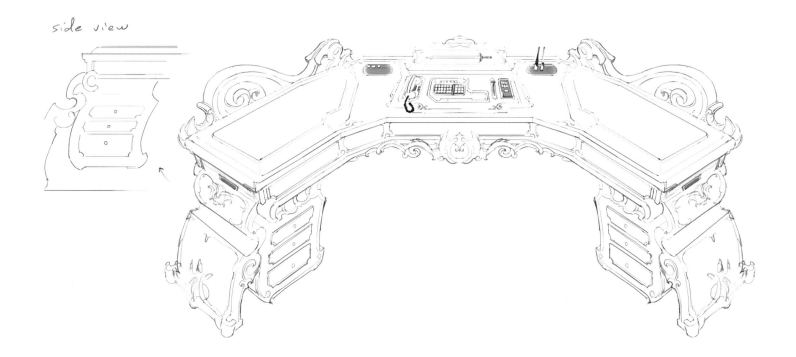

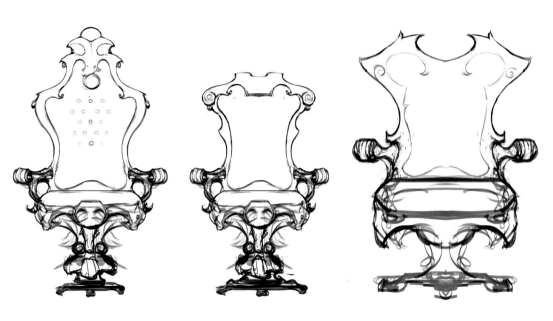

Mengsk's chair went through many design iterations and its final form resembles a throne.

ABOVE
Color scripts showing the death of Mengsk.

RIGHT
Early concept art of this scene. The staging would change dramatically for the final version.

ABOVE AND RIGHT
Concept sketches and
color scripts showing
the death of Mengsk and
Kerrigan's ascendance.

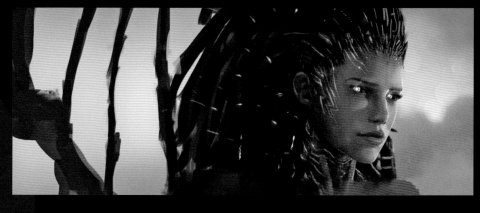

ABOVE AND RIGHT
Concept sketches and
color scripts showing
the death of Mengsk and
Kerrigan's ascendance.

THE END OF *HEART OF THE SWARM* WAS THE
final reckoning of conflicts that began almost fifteen
years earlier during the 1998 release of *StarCraft*.
The betrayal of Sarah Kerrigan by Arcturus Mengsk
created a monster, and that monster had returned
for vengeance.

Despite all of his plans, schemes, and tricks, nothing
could save Arcturus Mengsk from her wrath.

This cinematic went through more revisions than
perhaps any other moment in the entire *StarCraft II*
saga. It had been identified as the climax of the zerg
campaign very early in the development process, and
work began on it long before Wings of Liberty had
been finished.

One particularly tricky moment was the death of
Arcturus Mengsk. Kerrigan filled him with raw power
and energy so strong that the Emperor quite literally
exploded.

To sell the illusion of power building inside him, the
cinematics team made unconventional use of a
common technique called subsurface scattering.
Normally, this helps simulate the way external light
gets diffused on skin—a key part of making 3-D
rendered skin look real.

For Mengsk, the technique was applied differently.
Not only were there external lights within the scene—
including glowing television screens just behind his
head—but now there was a new and lethal light
building inside of his brain. Making both lights play
together was tricky, but the effect came out looking
remarkably painful.

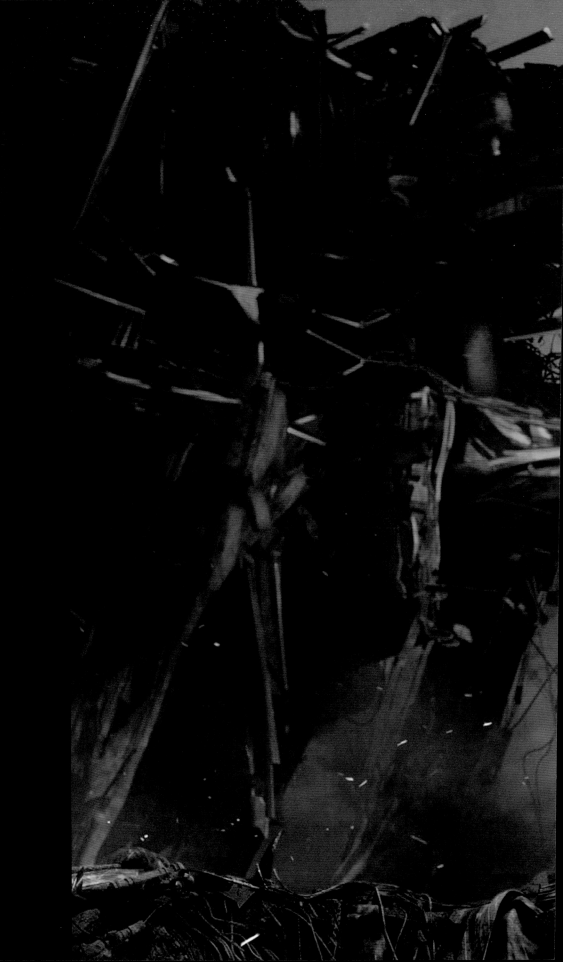

THE ENDING OF *HEART OF THE SWARM* **DELIBERATELY** called back to the ending of *Wings of Liberty*—both in staging and in tone. Raynor carrying Kerrigan into the sunset had suggested that maybe . . . just maybe . . . there might be a happy ending for them somewhere in this story.

The events of the second chapter in the *StarCraft II* trilogy made it clear that Kerrigan's true enemy was not Arcturus Mengsk, but the dark force seeking to claim the entire galaxy. Once her vengeance was complete, Kerrigan and Raynor made peace with that. And so, under the Korhal sky—which was designed to look similar to the sunset on Char—Raynor let her go.

If there was going to be a happy ending, it would have to wait for another day.

3

LEGACY OF THE VOID

THE TERRAN REVOLUTION TO OVERTHROW DICTATOR ARCTURUS MENGSK REACHED ITS END. WHILE THE HEROES OF RAYNOR'S RAIDERS STRUGGLED TO REFORM a corrupt government, the protoss were preparing to reclaim their shattered homeworld.

The unified protoss, now known as the "Daelaam," had joined together to assault their zerg-infested homeworld of Aiur. Once the shining crown of the protoss empire, it was now the ruined consequence of the great race's arrogance.

The legendary warrior Artanis, chosen by ranking protoss as their Hierarch, commanded both the Khalai and Nerazim fleets to retake Aiur.

But as Artanis prepared for the invasion, the dark templar mystic Zeratul continued his hunt for answers, hoping that he could find the key to salvation for the galaxy.

And believing that Artanis was about to make a terrible mistake.

IT WAS THE BEGINNING OF THE END. *LEGACY OF the Void* was set to provide closure to the mysterious prophecies and portends of cosmic doom that had been teased as early as *Brood War*. The proud, advanced protoss would carry the torch for the final installment of the *StarCraft II* trilogy, and thus, they needed a suitable reintroduction.

The previous *StarCraft II* expansions had focused heavily on the conflict between various terran factions and the zerg Swarm. Zeratul had popped up from time to time, but players had so far only seen brief glimpses of the other major protoss characters in the saga.

The announcement cinematic for *Legacy of the Void* needed to remind people why the protoss were so dangerous, so determined . . . and so awesome. If the *Heart of the Swarm* cinematic had shown the pinnacle zerg fantasy—overrunning layers of defense with overwhelming numbers—then this cinematic needed to showcase the protoss fantasy: triumphing over those overwhelming numbers.

THE CINEMATIC ART OF **STARCRAFT**

THE ORIGINAL *STARCRAFT* HAD SHOWN A limited view of the protoss homeworld. Aiur had been under siege, in ruins, and occupied by the zerg, Overmind. For *Legacy of the Void*, the team now had the time and technology to show so much more than what was possible in 1998. Concept and environment artists spent months searching for the right aesthetic to communicate the grandeur of what the all-important homeworld once was.

Most early ideas for this scene centered around the ruins of Aiur's once-great cities. One approach staged the battle in the shadow of a collapsed protoss nexus. Another planned to have crumbling warp gates in the background.

To show depth in the location, the cinematics team decided to use a destroyed carrier for the backdrop, rather than a wrecked building. Crashed and gutted, the carrier was big enough to display protoss technology on a massive scale while also allowing many shots to stretch out to the horizon.

Other early concepts called for the land to be covered in "creep," the expanding purple biomass that serves as a living boundary of the zerg's territory. But the reality of covering every piece of terrain in a pulsating fleshy mass was more trouble than it was worth, and the result would have looked more "odd" than "awesome."

The final look of the environment was based off the barren landscapes of the far northern latitudes on Earth, especially the tundras of Greenland and the Arctic.

DESIGNING PROTOSS CHARACTERS FOR THIS cinematic offered interesting challenges for modelers and lighting artists.

The power suits of the protoss zealots were elaborate, reflective, and dinged-up from previous battles, but still needed to have that unmistakable "golden" look. For certain shots, the glow of their psi blades needed to cast light on both the zealot and the zerg creature they were fighting.

The high templar armor proved especially difficult. Not only did artists have the same difficulties as the zealot design, but the high templar armor needed to look significantly more ornate. Additionally, a cloth cape had to be simulated for every shot.

These challenges increased dramatically for the "bullet-time" sequence early in the cinematic. As a pack of zerg ambushed a group of templar from below, time slowed to a crawl. Ripples of blue light traveled from the nerve cords of one warrior to the others—demonstrating the connection the protoss had to each other through the Khala.

When depicting time moving so slowly, every object that responded to the laws of physics—the cloth of a high templar's cape, pieces of dirt kicked up during the ambush, saliva dripping from a hydralisk's maw—required exponentially greater resources for simulation. The rendering time for each frame became downright painful.

HIGH TEMPLAR
CONCEPT BY ANTHONY JONES

PROBE

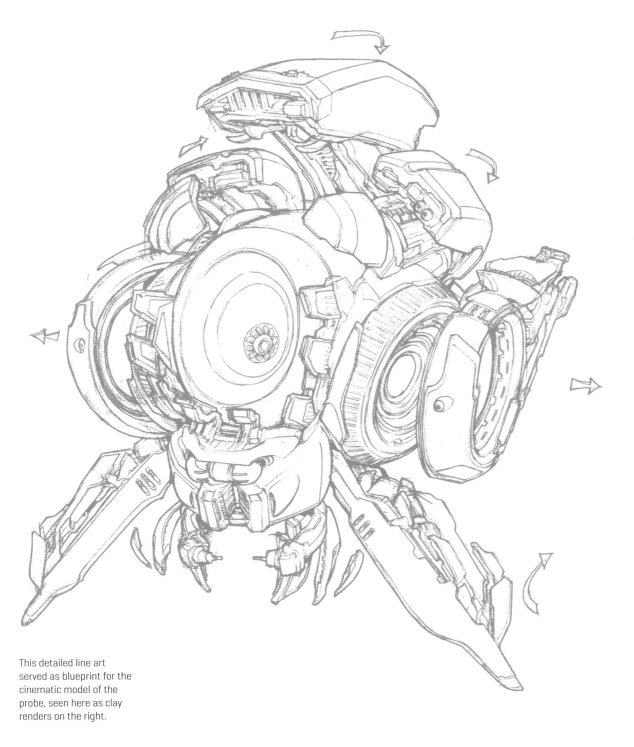

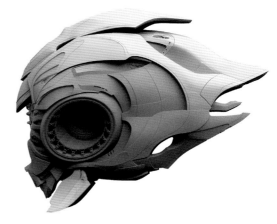

This detailed line art served as blueprint for the cinematic model of the probe, seen here as clay renders on the right.

PROTOSS PROBES HAD NEVER BEEN SHOWN IN cinematic form before. After many design concepts, this little robot ended up being modeled from the inside out. Even though it was only seen in a few shots, many of its parts moved and shifted in a way that allowed the audience to see inside its chassis.

A few years after the cinematic released, this particular probe was given a name—Probius—by the *Heroes of the Storm* team and was included as a playable character in their game.

The protoss colossus towe
over the battlefield, so it is
important to establish its s
relative to creatures like a
protoss zealot.

Artists spent considerable time making the colossus in the cinematics mimic the look of the in-game unit.

THE ART OF PROCEDURAL GENERATION—A process of creating elements through well-crafted systems rather than hand-designing every molecule of a moment—was used in several stylized shots within this cinematic.

The exploding baneling with its burst of caustic slime and the zealot's fracturing shield are all elements that were created using procedural systems.

The end of the cinematic showed dozens of zealots "warping in" to the battlefield—essentially appearing out of nowhere. The vertical flash of light and the "digitizing" style of the teleportation were generated procedurally so it would not look like a cloned effect, but rather a process that was happening for each individual warrior.

The last major use of procedural generation came when two high templar merged into a powerful archon. Technical artists built and tweaked a system that simulated the destruction of the two protoss bodies before their merging, making it appear as though they were being ripped apart molecule by molecule.

As the archon appeared on the battlefield (another procedurally generated effect), it soon began a hand-to-hand fight with a massive ultralisk.

Through repeated iterations in 2-D storyboards and 3-D pre-visualization, the cinematics team carefully staged the battle in a way that showed the two huge creatures ripping each other to pieces against the wreckage of a destroyed protoss carrier.

The ultralisk model was rebuilt from the *Heart of the Swarm* introduction cinematic, but the archon model was built from scratch. Artists focused on making the shape of its armor huge and easy to read at a distance, while allowing room for intricate levels of detail in close-ups. This was key to making sure both creatures felt several stories tall and weighed hundreds of tons each.

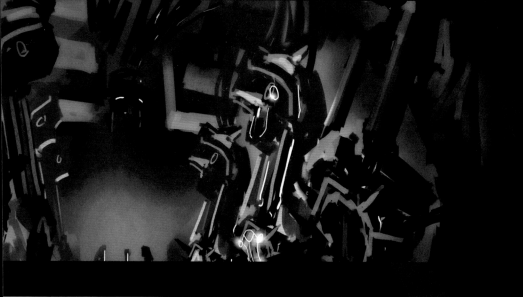

"WHAT CAUSE COULD
BE MORE NOBLE THAN
RECLAIMING OUR HOME?"
—KALDALIS

ABOVE
Concepts showing the
sacred resting place of
the xel'naga.

LEFT
Line sketch showing the
scale of a protoss city and
its vehicles.

BY THE TIME PRODUCTION HAD WRAPPED ON
Legacy of the Void, the cinematics team had been
working on pre-rendered and in-game cinematics for
almost a decade. A tremendous amount of creative
and technical collaboration had resulted in a suite of
in-engine cinematic features that dwarfed what was
available in the early days of *Wings of Liberty*.

Which was good, since the in-game cutscenes for
Legacy of the Void were by far the most ambitious
cinematics attempted within the saga.

"AIUR IS OUR PAST,
BUT IS IT OUR FUTURE?"
– Artanis

THE FIRST IN-GAME CINEMATIC OF THE CAMPAIGN
showed Hierarch Artanis giving a rousing speech to
the Golden Armada, and commanding them to initiate
the long-awaited reclamation of their homeworld.
Ranks of protoss warriors were packed onto every
warp platform in the fleet, and in the background,
Aiur itself was lit by the rising sun.

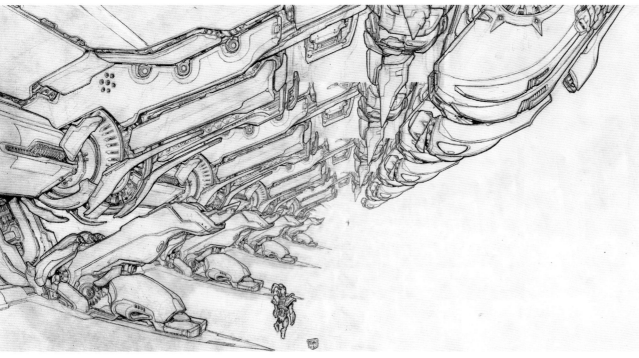

These mothership concept pieces were originally drawn on paper—very large sheets of paper—and then scanned into the computer.

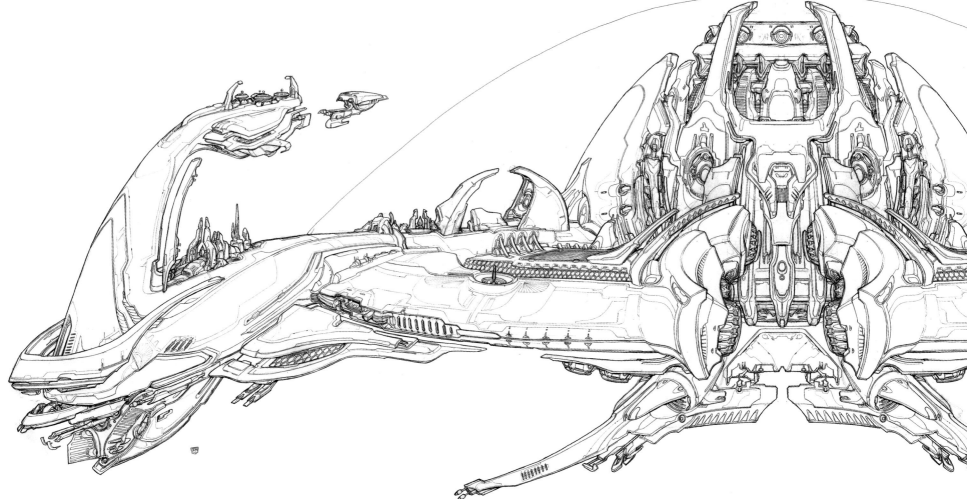

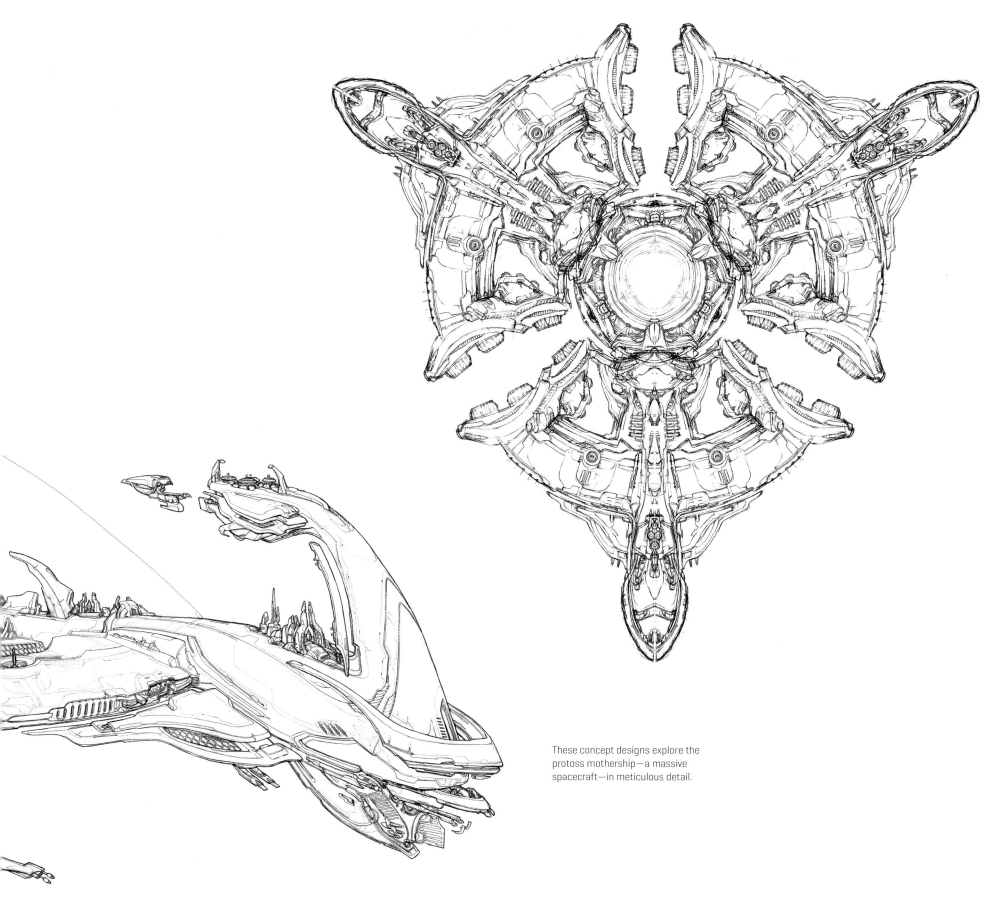

These concept designs explore the protoss mothership—a massive spacecraft—in meticulous detail.

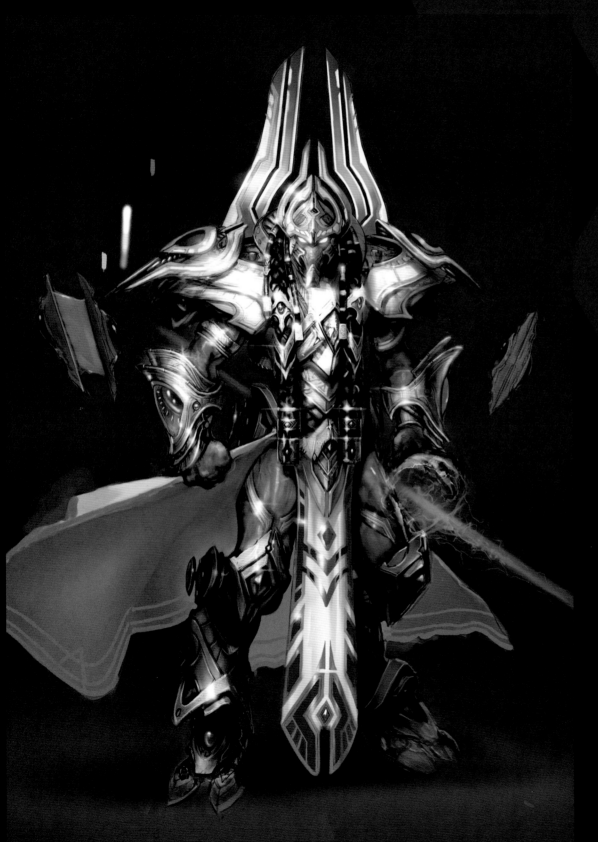

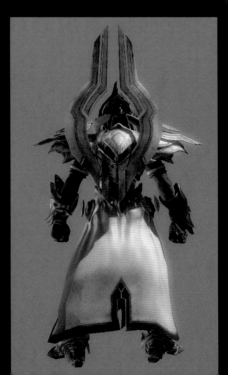

Artanis's detailed concept
art (far left) is faithfully
translated to his 3-D
model (close left).

THE SHEER NUMBER OF CHARACTER MODELS, objects, and sets required to execute scenes were far beyond anything the team had ever done. Even simple dialogue exchanges between Artanis and Zeratul required multiple warriors standing at the ready and holding their blades out in the background of every scene.

Protoss do not have mouths, so animators did not have to account for lip-syncing in many of *Legacy of the Void*'s scenes. However, this wasn't much of a relief: humans rely heavily on lip movements to understand a character's emotions. (Blizzard's statistics indicate most of its players are human.) Animators had to exaggerate protoss body language so their "performances" would be clear.

BEFORE LONG, THE MARCH ON AIUR DESCENDED into disaster. The dark god, Amon, seized control of the Khala and all the protoss still connected to it . . . including Hierarch Artanis.

The only one that could save him was Zeratul. But at a price.

The confrontation between Zeratul and the possessed Hierarch drew inspiration from classic samurai movies, which influenced the choreography, pacing, and composition of many shots. The fight needed to show more than an action scene; it needed to show the tragic consequence of Artanis's decision to reclaim Aiur, and the beginning of his heroic journey.

The climax of the cinematic—when Zeratul willingly accepts a fatal blow while severing Artanis's nerve cords—required special modeling attention. Artanis's cords were simulated separately, then seamlessly attached to his base character and treated with subtle deformation effects to make them appear as if they stretched slightly before coming apart. With the addition of some post-production lightning and heat effects, artists created the impression that Zeratul's blades had just struck their mark.

Zeratul sacrificed himself for the hero he knew could save the galaxy from Amon's wrath. It was a fitting send-off for perhaps one of the most widely-known characters in *StarCraft*'s long history.

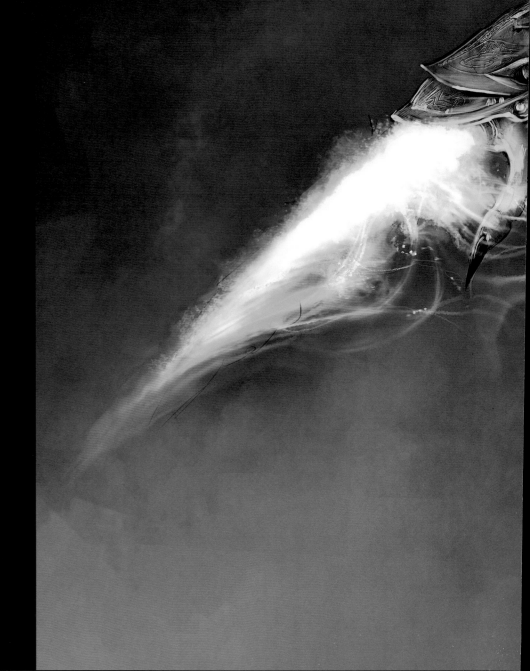

WITHOUT THE KHALA, ARTANIS FELT CUT OFF from his own people. His way of life was gone. Instead of submitting to despair, Artanis turned to the wisdom of the dark templar. After a massive zerg attack within the heart of Shakuras, Matriarch Vorazun honored his decision to put the needs of the many before his own and welcomed Artanis on the path of the Nerazim.

Artanis's solitary battle against an onslaught of zerg was also a complex action sequence that required months of storyboard work and several more months of production to complete. Between the nydus worm bursting through a wall, the waves of zerglings and hydralisks swarming over Artanis, the psionic storm that hurled dozens of zerglings through the air, and the exploding planet, the demands of this cutscene could have easily made the project impossible to complete on time.

The success of this cinematic was proof of the many valuable lessons learned throughout the production of the *StarCraft II saga*. The entire team now had a firm grasp on how to achieve each insane action moment through animation, rigging, texturing, lighting, post-production effects, and editing.

Without the experience of the cinematics team and the production staff, a cutscene of this complexity would never have been possible to make on time.

Especially when there were several more scenes of equal complexity left to do.

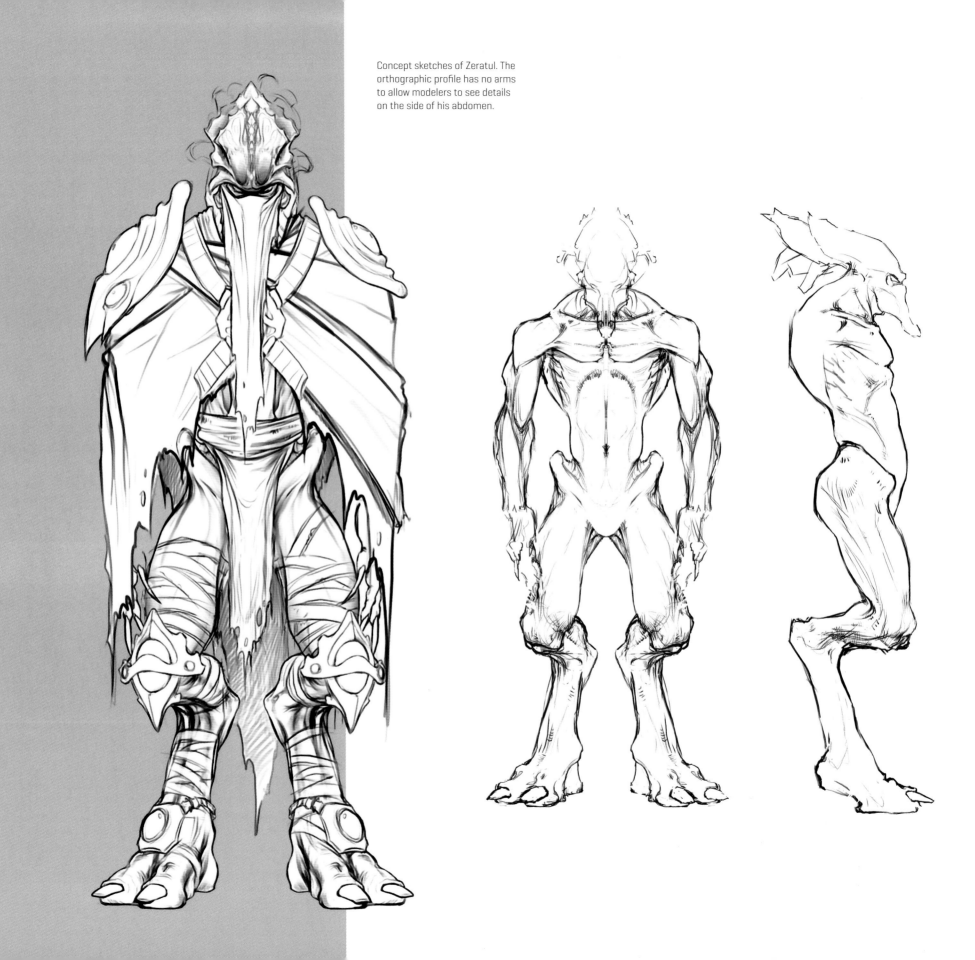

Concept sketches of Zeratul. The orthographic profile has no arms to allow modelers to see details on the side of his abdomen.

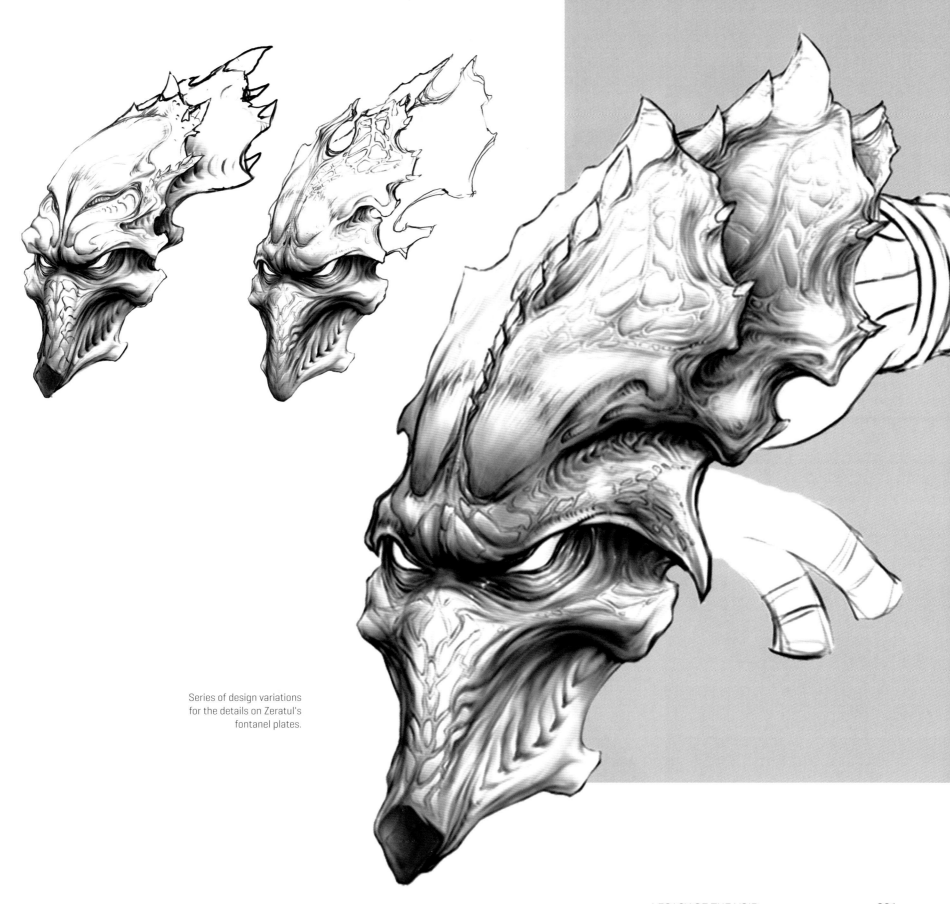

Series of design variations
for the details on Zeratul's
fontanel plates.

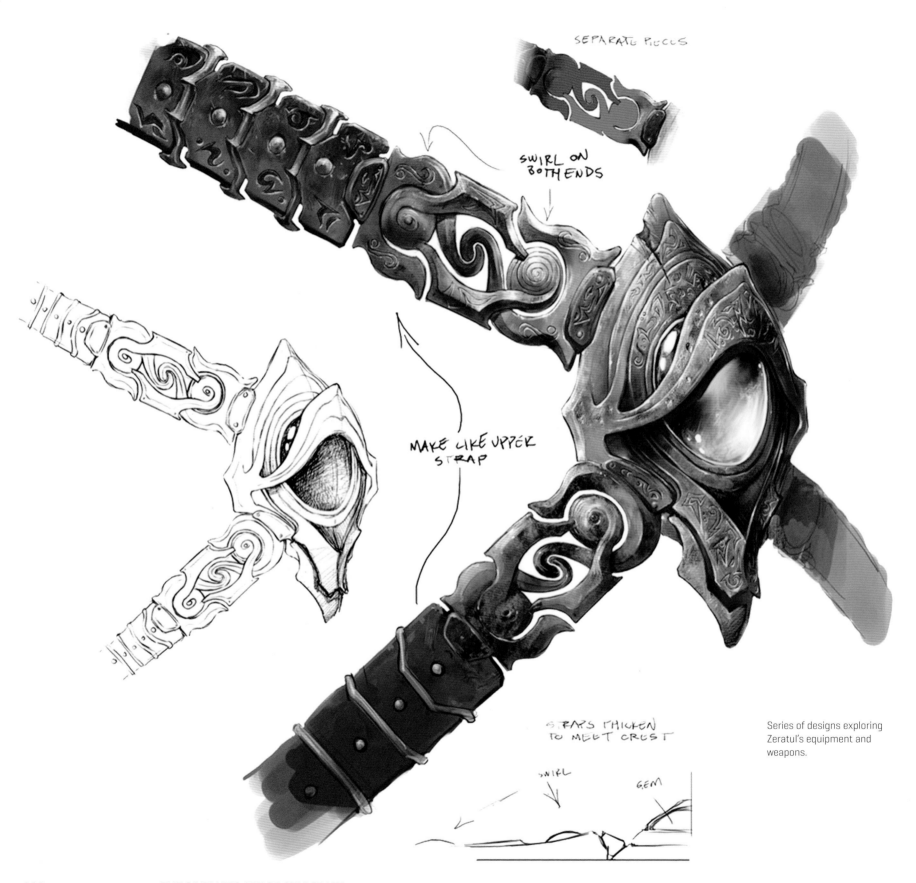

SEPARATE PIECES

SWIRL ON BOTH ENDS

MAKE LIKE UPPER STRAP

STRAPS THICKEN TO MEET CREST

SWIRL

GEM

Series of designs exploring Zeratul's equipment and weapons.

The final look for Zeratul's wrist gauntlet (right) was the result of many design iterations.

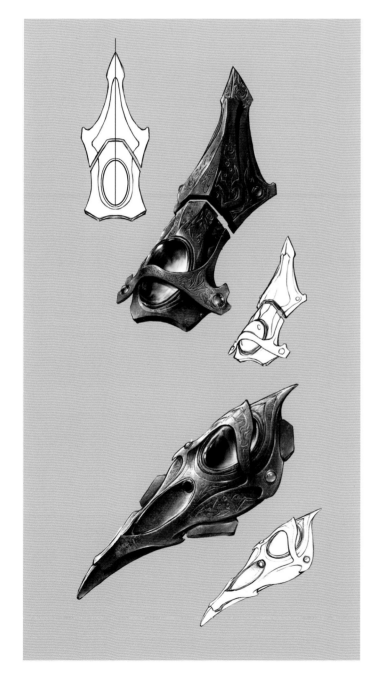

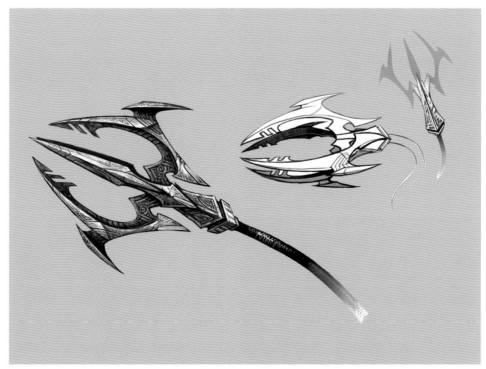

"WITHOUT THE KHALA,
WHAT WILL WE
BECOME?"
—SELENDIS

"FREE."
—ARTANIS

THE LAST MISSION IN *LEGACY OF THE VOID*'S
campaign began with a speech from the Hierarch
that challenged all protoss factions—the Khalai, the
Nerazim, and the Tal'darim—to discard their old
prejudices and form a new civilization based on unity.

The final proof of Artanis's leadership didn't come
from a display of warrior skill, but from persuading his
people to let go of their past and believe in his vision
for a better future.

The effect of "persuasion" was difficult to animate
when the characters did not have mouths.

The complex animation rigs for the protoss—built with
features developed for the last ten years—had put
a considerable amount of importance on the facial
features around the eyes. Characters like Executor
Selendis needed to show a range of emotions in
this scene: uncontrollable rage when she was under
control of Amon, confusion and weariness when his
power was interrupted, and steely-eyed resolve when
she chose to cut her own nerve cords.

Ultimately, those emotions could only be represented
through subtle movements in her brow, cheeks,
glowing pupils, and body language. Attention to detail
and careful animation allowed these small features
to do the emotional heavy-lifting, making the scene
read naturally.

The look of Selendis's armor and equipment had many iterations before settling on her final design (lower image).

More experiments with Selendis's design, including explorations of an elaborate custom weapon (later removed).

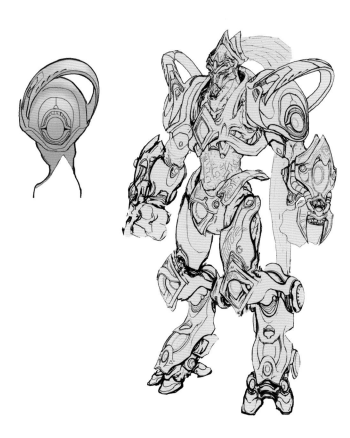

Sketches and color art showing an updated design for the zealot.

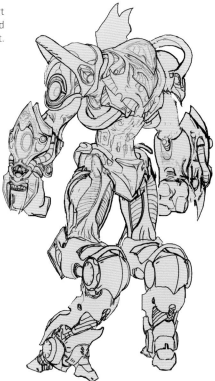

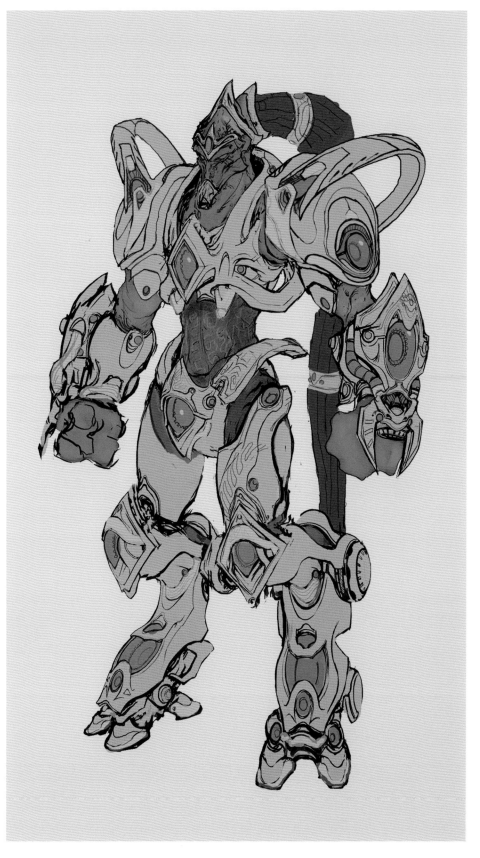

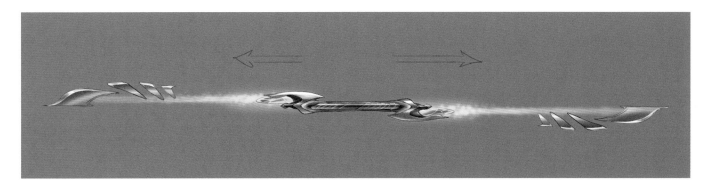

LEFT
Concept art of Selendis, the executor of the protoss.

RIGHT
An early concept of Selendis's weapon.

BELOW
An acrylic concept painting of a protoss immortal.

Very early concepts exploring
Amon's most powerful minions:
the hybrid.

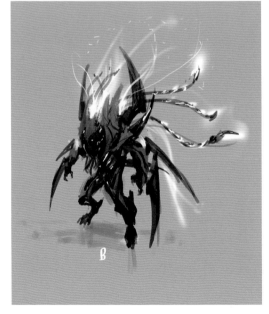

Since the hybrids are created from both protoss and zerg, concept artists explored many ideas of how they could be depicted. Some versions are clearly insectoid and zerg, while others have more of a protoss design and a warrior's stance.

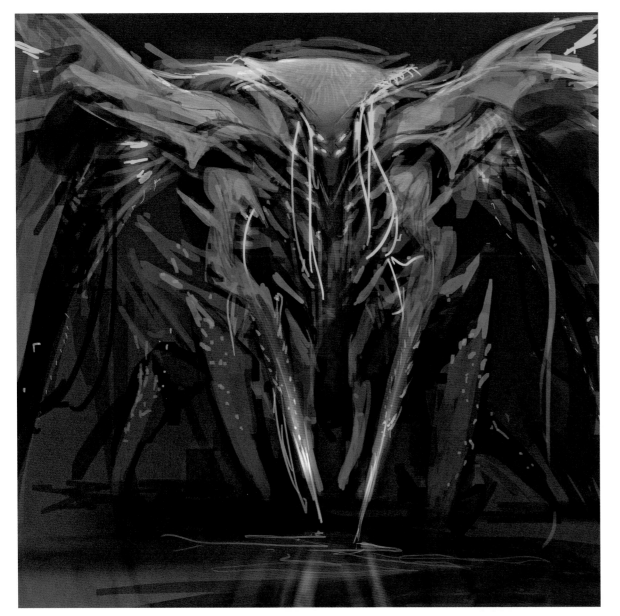

Since the hybrid would be seen both in the game and in the cinematics, they needed to be identifiable in either.

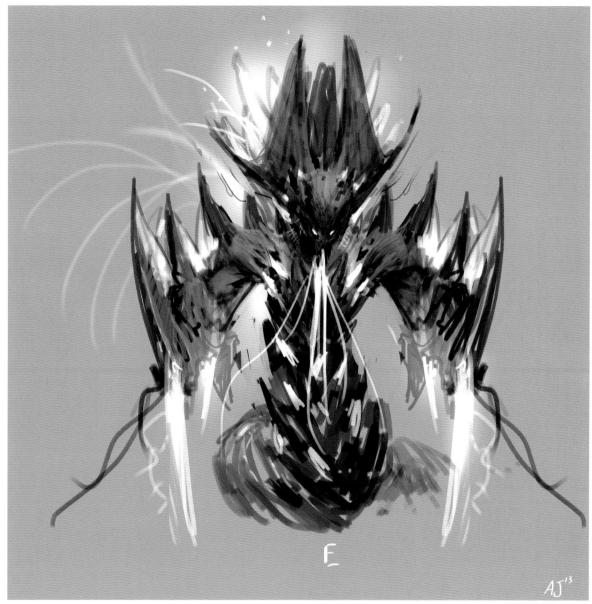

These pieces highlight the glowing, corrupted power from some of the hybrid's earlier designs.

Legacy of the Void is the first time Amon has been shown in all his power and glory.

A lengthy design process with many iterations helped determine how Amon—and the other xel'naga—should look.

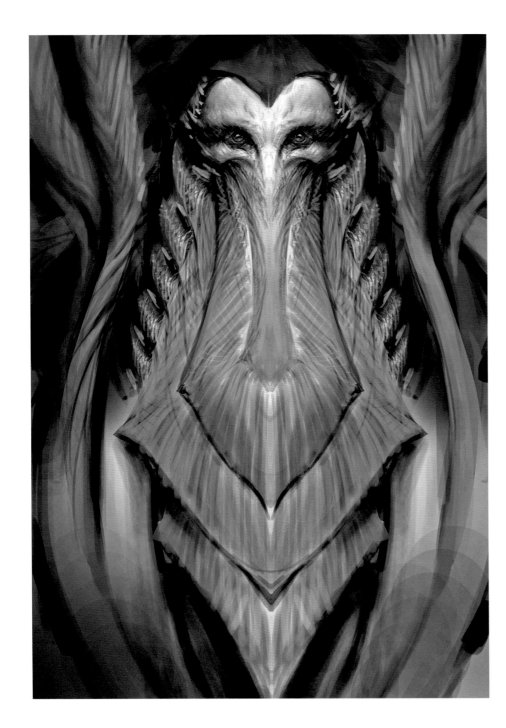

Amon's different design concepts range from regal and powerful to something significantly more monstrous.

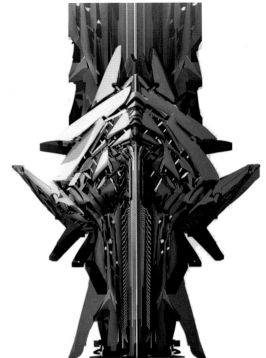

The final resting place of the xel'naga needed to be iconic in silhouette and shape. Concept art helps explore what the tomb of the xel'naga might have looked like before it was ravaged.

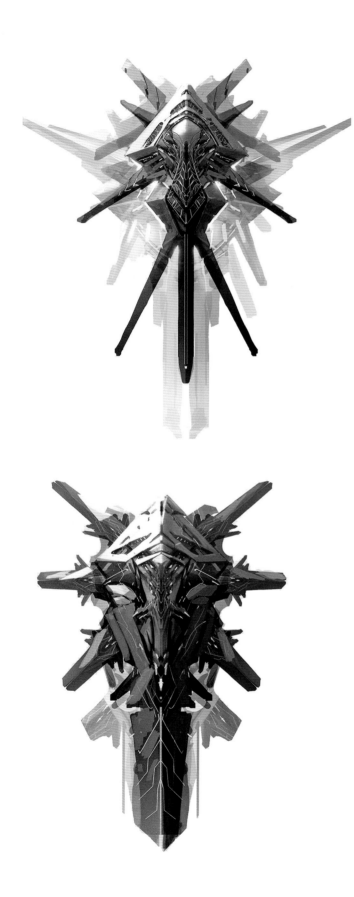

"IT SEEMS FATE HAS DRAWN US TOGETHER. WE SHOULD NOT TEMPT IT FURTHER."
—Artanis

WHEN A LIVE-ACTION CAMERA MOVES FROM A dimly lit indoor space to full sunlight, the outdoors look "blown-out" because the extreme contrast in brightness overwhelms all other details. This effect is frequently considered a mistake. But, like other kinds of mistakes (a "lens flare," for example), it can be used intentionally for dramatic effect.

Each part of the *StarCraft II* saga used this approach, often to show characters entering or leaving a scene. When Artanis and Kerrigan came face-to-face with the might of Amon's power in the tomb of the xel'naga, the space beyond the massive opening door was so bright that it created the blown-out effect. This served to create a feeling of something epic beyond the door for Artanis and Kerrigan to confront.

In addition to creating dramatic lighting, the blown-out effect also guarded against disasters in production. Cinematics and mission maps were not always completed at the same time; the effect meant that cinematic artists didn't need to build their virtual set "outside," and game artists still had the freedom to imagine what was outside in the way that best served the game.

THE CINEMATIC ART OF **STARCRAFT**

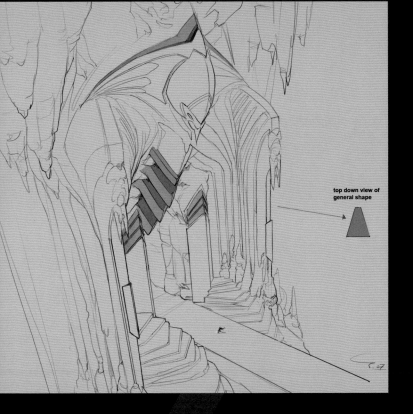

top down view of
general shape

A series of concept
images help define the
look of the xel'naga's
tomb on Ulnar, with a lone
warrior approaching the
entrance for scale.

Other concepts for Ulnar show impressions of xel'naga faces staring down on anyone who enters.

More concept art of Ulnar's environment exploring different styles of architecture and unique formations inside the underground complex.

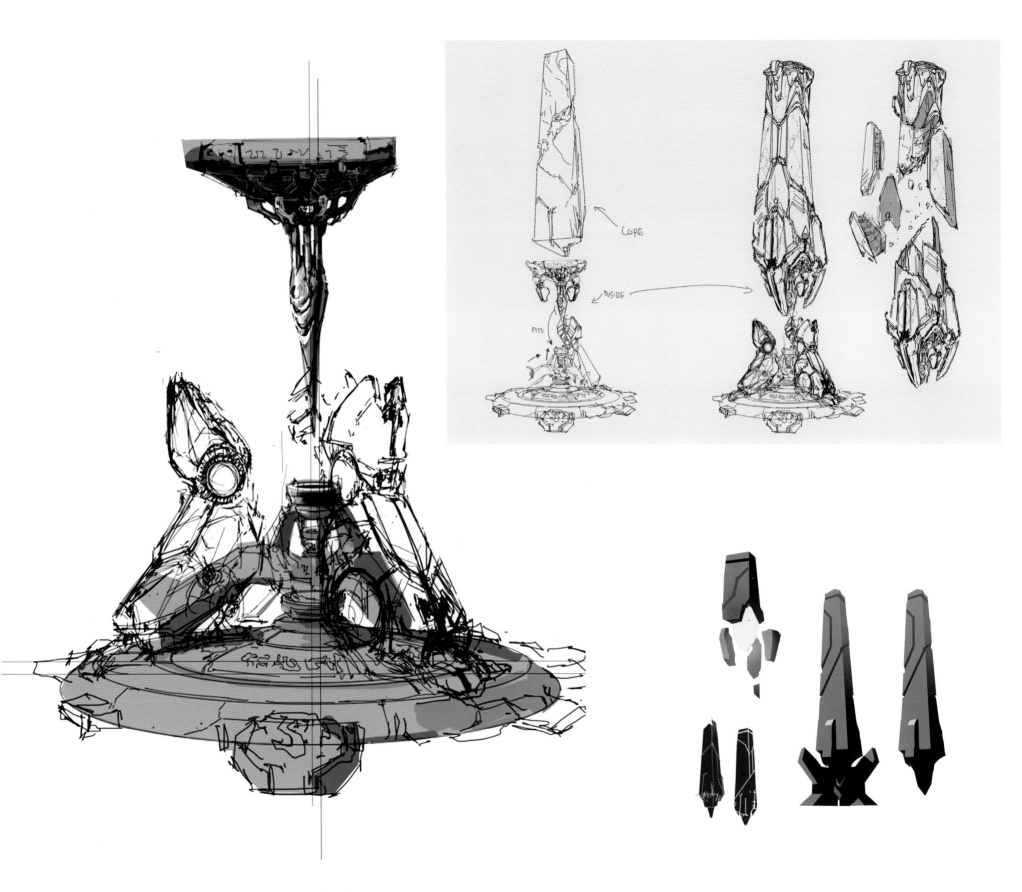

THE CINEMATIC ART OF **STARCRAFT**

Different examples of xel'naga architecture appear across all three expansions. Countless iterations were required to make sure each expansion has recognizable—but still unique—environments.

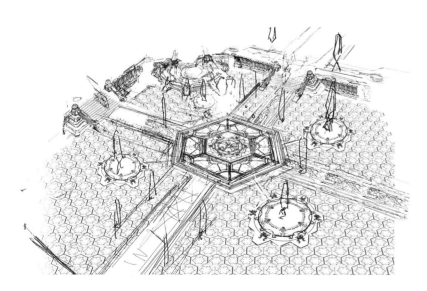

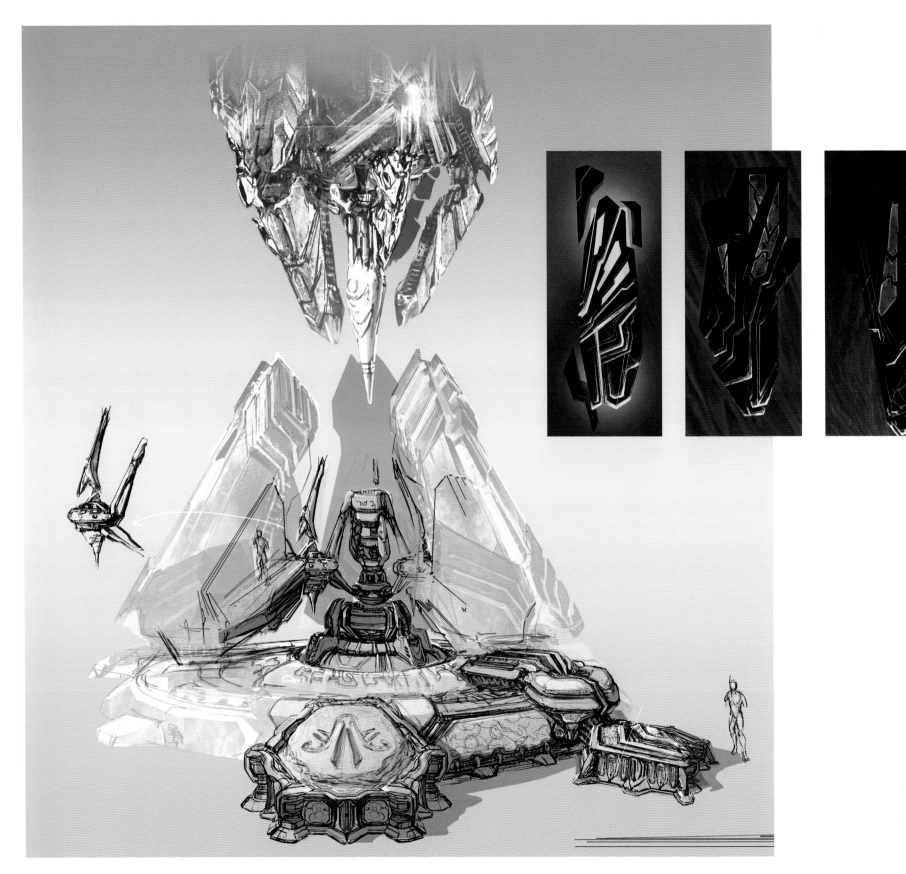

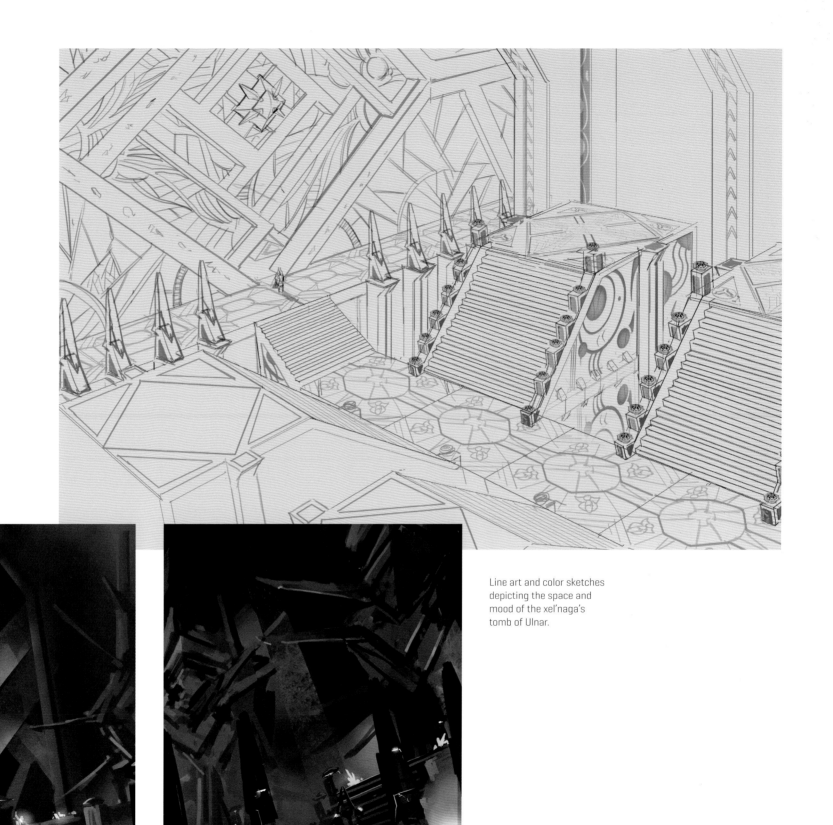

Line art and color sketches depicting the space and mood of the xel'naga's tomb of Ulnar.

The final versions of the hybrid were designed as nightmarish creatures wielding Amon's dark power. These drawings show their anatomy in great detail.

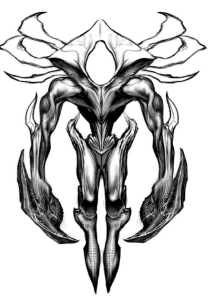

"WE WILL GATHER THE SURVIVORS . . .
REBUILD OUR CITIES. WE WILL
REJECT OUR OLD DIVISIONS AND
FORGE A NEW SOCIETY. TOGETHER,
WE WILL SHAPE OUR DESTINY
AMONGST THE STARS."

—ARTANIS

VICTORIOUS, THE PROTOSS BEGAN TO REBUILD
their civilization on Aiur. This was represented by an
eighteen-second time-lapse shot showing a new city
coming to life over a period of several days.

This was the first time the cinematics team had ever
attempted a time-lapse shot. Even in real life, time-
lapse footage looks inherently unrealistic. That was
both good and bad.

"It meant nobody could tell us we were doing it wrong,
but nobody could tell us how to do it right," said
cinematic artist David Luong.

Unlike the other shots in the cinematic, this sequence
was not built with the game engine. Using the workflow
for larger pre-rendered works (such as the *Legacy
of the Void* introduction cinematic), a small team of
artists carefully assembled the required ingredients:
buildings, terrain, clouds and planets, a day-to-night-
to-day lighting cycle, and the streaking lights of probes
zipping around at nighttime.

The result was one of the most unique shots in the
entire saga.

The final missions of the "Into the Void" epilogue reveal the true form of the xel'naga and show Kerrigan's ascension into one.

The cosmic depiction of the xel'naga
went through several iterations but
always maintained their massive size.

THE END OF *LEGACY OF THE VOID* FREED THE
protoss from Amon's grasp, but it did not destroy
him completely. After the development of the
campaign was underway, the storytellers on both the
cinematics and game teams decided that it would be
too easy to pair the salvation of the protoss with the
death of Amon.

The epilogue missions of *StarCraft II* had the
commanders of all three races joining together for
a final strike into the Void, the realm where Amon
resided. His fate, and the fate of the universe itself,
would be decided in a series of epic battles and
cinematics. These final moments would end the
threat of Amon, fulfill the ultimate plan of the xel'naga,
and complete the destiny of Sarah Kerrigan.

Wish you were here

TWO YEARS
LATER . . .

THE FINAL IN-GAME CINEMATIC FOR *STARCRAFT II* hearkened back to the game's very first cutscene. Just like in *Wings of Liberty*, Jim Raynor was drinking at Joey Ray's Bar and watching the news when someone darkened the doorway and changed his life. But instead of kicking a revolution into overdrive, this person brought the happy ending that Raynor never believed he'd get—Sarah Kerrigan.

The scene was deliberately lit with a surreal glow. Kerrigan had ascended to a state beyond mortal comprehension. She was no longer merely human or zerg, but xel'naga. Raynor set down his old marshal badge and laid his heroics to rest. Now he could be with his long-lost love, regardless of her form.

Amon was gone. The Swarm had pulled back to Char and the Terran Dominion began peace talks with the united protoss. Life began anew on formerly decimated planets. The war-torn Koprulu sector could finally rest easy.

For a time.

"4TH ANNUAL HYDRALISK DERBY, 1ST PLACE BABY!"

TIRED OF LIFE ?

call 777-303
for assignments to first wave
marine landing teams !!

DOMINION PUBLIC ANNOUNCEMENT

BY REQUEST OF THE KEL-MORIAN COMBINE, ALL SECURITY ON THE
WORLD OF MAR SARA IS NOW THE RESPONSIBILITY OF THE TERRAN
DOMINION

over, my dead cold body!! WHATEVER DUDE

ALL CITIZENS ARE SUBJECT TO IMMEDIATE SEARCH AND UNLIMITED
DETENTION ON SUSPICION OF ANY OF THE FOLLOWING CRIMES-

ILLEGAL ASSEMBLY
UNAUTHORIZED COMMNUNICATIONS
RECIDIVISM
HOARDING
TAX EVASION
PROPERTY DAMAGE
RESOURCE PIRACY
AIDING AND ABETTING A KNOWN FELON
CRIMINAL ASSOCIATION
WEAPONS VIOLATIONS
FAILURE TO DISCLOSE ILLCIT ACTIVITY
IMPEDING A DOMINION PEACEKEEPER IN THEIR DUTIES

SCREW YOU

YEAH!!

MENGSK!!

EXTRA — The Mar Sa...

Vol CCXXIV, No. 3516   MAR SARA

LOCAL REBEL
SAVES COLONISTS

Winning Hearts and Minds-The Evolution of Revolution

By Richard Astley

When the aptly named Meteor Station suffered a critical strike on their processing units the outlook was grim. The nearest help was a week away and the eight hundred-odd colonists and crew on the station had less than 48 hours of breathable air. Things seemed to have only gotten worse when an unregistered warship prowled in out of the churning mass of rock surrounding the station – Pirates? Aliens? Worse?

Jim Raynor rescues an orphan out of burning building

...it turned out the grim, battle-scarred ship was to be their salvation. It was the ship of Jim Raynor, a notorious rebel, setting aside his ongoing war with the Terran Dominion to help out some people in trouble. Thanks to him and his colorful crew the station was saved and eight hundred souls were not consigned to eternal silence of the void. He never asked for acknowledgement or payment of any kind, he and his men simply took care of the problem and left happy that they could make a difference – a hard act to reconcile with the bloody handed terrorist portrayed on UNN. But where did this man's war with Dominion begin? And why has he persisted with an impossible fight down the years, constantly moving from world to world and spreading dissension in his wake?

It was easy to miss. The Confederacy was dying before our eyes, the zerg were overrunning world after world, the once terrorist supremo and soon-to-be Emperor Arcturus Mengsk was emerging as

Amidst all this fire and fury one man and a handful of his ardent supporters turned their backs on the Sons of Korhal and Arcturus Mengsk, stealing Mengsk's own flagship, the Hyperion, and disappeared into space.

They declared Mengsk a tyrant, a worse leader than the corrupt old families of the Confederacy. On the very eve of victory that one man, an ex-marshal from the badlands of Mar Sara by the name of Jim Raynor, rejected the very revolution he had helped to make into a reality.

abczbzba
abcbzba
aagad
shdf
hxcv

hey
ygi
dn
jgl
jhg
v,

NEW SPECIES OF AMPHIBIAN
DISCOVERED- ATTACKS TOWN

By Horbert George Wales

Last night a resupply convoy was attacked by large bipedal ichthyoids off the coast of Viewport Beach. Survivors report smelling a peculiar odor before the ambush, which left

A team of exterminators quicky ended the th... burning all the vermin. Screams of "MMMR... MRGLMRGL!" were heard all throughout night... ...ile juvenile specimen was ta...

50¢   **The Sentin...**

Vol. XLII, No. 301 **K   SUNDAY, MARCH 18, 2500

RAYNOR'S RAIDERS:
EVOLUTION OF REVOLUTION

It was easy to miss. The Confederacy was dying before our eyes, the zerg were overrunning world after world, the once terrorist supremo and soon-to-be Emperor Arcturus Mengsk was emerging as the unlikely saviour of the tottering remnants of humanity. Amidst all this fire and fury one man and a handful of his ardent supporters turned their backs on the Sons of Korhal and Arcturus Mengsk, stealing Mengsk's own flagship, the Hyperion, and disappeared into space. They declared Mengsk a tyrant, a worse leader than the corrupt old families of the Confederacy. On the very eve of victory that one man, an ex-marshal from the badlands of Mar Sara by the name of Jim Raynor, rejected the very revolution he had helped to make into a reality. Why?

by MIKE LIBERTY

SKULL CUT FROM FABRIC
& STITCHED ON—

SOMEWHAT SLOPPY CUTS (AGES
PAST A BIT, I.E. CUT W/ SCISSORS)

[STARCRAFT2 IN-GAME][VOODOO DOLL]
[HORNER VICTORY CINEMATIC]

DYLAR SHIP YARDS

"where caca happens baby..."

JOIN now!

I WANT YOU FOR THE

ARMORY BOWLING TEAM

BAR B Q
picnic 2.28
BRING THE FAMILY!
HOT DAMN!
LIVE MUSIC + DANCING
COURTESY OF PEABODY TUBTHUMPERS
DON'T FORGET YER FILTERBLOCK
AND R2BREATHER

JIM RAYNOR, OUR MOST FAMOUS PATRON

321ST COLONIAL RANGERS BATTALION, HEAVEN'S DEVILS

Over the past twenty years, hundreds of passionate professionals have offered their skills, imagination, and expertise to help create the unforgettable cinematics for *StarCraft*.

Thank you for your creativity, countless late nights of work, and commitment to making the impossible a reality. Everything we accomplished, we accomplished together.

Special thanks to the *StarCraft* development team, for creating games we will never forget, and for being such generous creative partners.

To everyone at Blizzard, your teamwork, tireless efforts, ideas, and feedback are what have made *StarCraft* the amazing game it is today.

Most importantly, thank you to the millions of players who have explored the Koprulu sector with us.

En taro StarCraft!

THE CINEMATIC ART OF
STARCRAFT®

BLIZZARD ENTERTAINMENT

WRITTEN BY
Robert Brooks

EDITORS
Allison Irons, Diandra Lasrado, Paul Morrissey, David Wohl

ART DIRECTION AND DESIGN
Chris Thunig

CREATIVE CONSULTATION
Jeff Chamberlain, Phillip Hillenbrand, Bridget O'Neill

LORE CONSULTATION
Sean Copeland, Christi Kugler, Justin Parker

PRODUCTION
Brianne M. Loftis, Timothy Loughran,
Alix Nicholaeff, Charlotte Racioppo, Derek Rosenberg,
Cara Samuelsen, Jeffrey Wong

DIRECTOR, CONSUMER PRODUCTS
Byron Parnell

DIRECTOR, CREATIVE DEVELOPMENT
Ralph Sanchez